HELEN KISH

The Artist and Her Dolls

HELEN KISH
The Artist and Her Dolls

Louise Fecher

Reverie

PUBLISHING COMPANY

First edition/First printing

To purchase additional copies of this book, please contact: Reverie Publishing Company, 130 South Wineow Street, Cumberland, MD 21502. 888-721-4999. www.reveriepublishing.com

Library of Congress Control Number 2006923665
ISBN 1-932485-36-8

Project Editor: Krystyna Poray Goddu
Design: Lynn Amos

Cover photo by Tamas Kish & Dan James: Veronica and Teddy (see page 113 for details)

Photo on page 2 by Tamas Kish & Dan James: White Woman (see page 85 for details)

Printed and bound in Korea

Contents

A family photo of Kish cuties includes, clockwise from left: Margie, Sophie, Riley, Petite Penelope (porcelain, 1984), Mary Kate and Kelsey.

The Helen Kish Story

The breadth of Helen Kish's artistic output is awe-inspiring. Her rich repertoire includes evocative one-of-a-kind sculptures made in clay, porcelain, bronze and stoneware; charming, limited-edition porcelain dolls that have been treasured by discerning collectors for more than twenty-five years; and award-winning vinyl dolls that are beloved by collectors of all ages around the globe.

Because of the variety of her creations, Helen Kish can be hard to characterize, even elusive. Like a butterfly, she is hard to catch. And just when you think you have her safe in your hands, to study and admire, she flutters away in a burst of spontaneity, eager to pursue another artistic path.

Yet, it is Helen's soaring flights of fancy that make her one of the most fascinating, sought-after and respected doll artists working today. She began working with clay and porcelain in the mid-1970s. Perfecting her skills as a maker of porcelain dolls was the artist's main path, yet she paused along the way to explore and master the mediums of bronze, stoneware clay and vinyl, the latter for which she has became best known. Helen has also sculpted whimsical, mixed-media pieces, made jewelry of precious metal and stones, and modeled bas-relief sculptures, figurines and plates.

Even more impressive than the artist's sweeping range is the seemingly effortless way that she glides back and forth along the sculptural spectrum, moving from one medium to the next, then back to the previous one, using her increased knowledge of one medium to enhance her skills in another.

"I don't have any trouble moving from one kind of work to another; but you have to understand, I'm certifiable," Helen confided in an interview with me in 2000. The self-described "compulsive sculptor" uses clay to record her thoughts and experiences the way others might use a journal or even a tape recorder. You or I might keep a notepad handy to jot down an idea; Helen Kish keeps a stash of clay near her bedroom in case she wakes up during the night and feels inspired. As she experiences life, her responses and emotions flow from

Portrait of Helen Kish, 2002

Combining beauty and artistry: African Madonna was made in 1988.

her mind to her steady hands, which in turn shape clay into forms that touch collectors' hearts, reminding us of the universal emotions that we all share.

Garden Girl, a resin bas-relief from 1995, is one of many expressions of the artist's creativity.

The Nalty Family

For many artists, the seeds of creativity are planted in childhood and nourished in youth. Helen Kish's artistic bent was certainly evident at an early age, but it took a back seat, first to her family's needs and beliefs, then to marriage and children. Yet, many of the family ties forged in Helen's childhood carved deep impressions that would later inspire many of her dolls. The artist's story thus begins with her birth, in 1950, to Donald and Doris Nalty.

Both natives of Colorado, Donald and Doris grew up in north Denver and knew each other as children. Donald graduated from high school in June 1942 and enlisted in the Navy that August at just seventeen years of age. While serving overseas, he began corresponding with Doris, who had begun working after her high school graduation. The pair began dating in 1946 when Donald returned to the United States, and wed in 1948.

"Before World War II, college was not an option for either of my parents, but Dad did take advantage of the GI bill after they married," Helen says. "Family lore is that the college girls wouldn't stop pursuing him—but really, work and family life got in the way—so he dropped out. Dad worked many different jobs early on: construction work, truck driver, plumber's assistant. But for most of my childhood until his retirement, Dad was a Colorado State Patrolman.

"He worked all the time, so we really didn't see a lot of him. My mother had to focus on the little ones, because there were always little ones that had to be taken care of," the artist recalls.

The couple's first child, Steve, was born in 1949. Next came Helen, followed by seven more children (one of whom died in infancy). "We were a big family, a pretty poor family, although I don't think we really knew that," the artist muses.

"The fifties and sixties were busy and stressful for us," the artist's father, Donald Nalty, recalled in an interview in early 2006. "Our family grew by leaps and bounds. I was scrambling to keep everything afloat by working extra jobs as much as possible. I often wished I had more free time to be with my children, as I knew I was missing out on a lot. And my wife was overburdened with the responsibilities of caring for the children."

From the time that Helen was born until she was about four years old, the Nalty family lived in Denver with Doris's mother, Mary Sillstrop ("a remarkable woman who came from a line of remarkable women," Helen says fondly) The same modest five-bedroom home was shared by one of Doris's sisters, her husband and their children.

By the time the fifth Nalty child arrived, Donald and Doris were able to purchase a small house in a suburb located southwest of Denver. And by the time the seventh baby came, the Naltys moved to a larger house that seemed luxurious at the time: a brand-new, three-bedroom ranch with a full basement. As the eldest girl, lucky Helen had her own bedroom, while sister Anne shared hers with the current baby sibling. The boys shared two rooms (and bunk beds) in the basement. "I lived there for the remainder of my childhood," the artist recalls.

Childhood Leanings and Longings

It is not unusual for a little girl to be passionate about her dolls, and Helen was no exception. As a toddler, she would fall asleep gazing at one of her first treasures: a rag doll from Poland, purchased by two beloved aunts— Aunt Marion ("Mai Mai") and Aunt Virginia ("Jiggie")— when Helen was born. Her favorite toy, received when she was five years old, was a jointed ballerina. (Worn but well loved, the doll resides in the artist's Denver home.)

In an unpublished interview from 2003 with author Krystyna Poray Goddu for her book *Dollmakers and Their Stories: Women Who Changed the World of Play* (Henry Holt and Co, 2004) the artist recalls her rather infamous discovery of the beautiful ballerina under the Christmas tree:

"My father was at work, and my mother stepped out to attend Christmas Eve Mass while a neighbor watched the house. I got up because I was so excited and I thought it was Christmas morning even though it was still dark outside. I thought, 'Oh well; it's still early.'

"I tried to wake up my brothers; my sister was only a year old so I didn't bother with her. But my brothers—there would have been three of them at that time—would not wake up. So I just got disgusted and went out to the tree and started to open the presents myself. I'd open one for one of the boys, and then I'd go back and try to tell them about it. But they wouldn't wake up, silly things!

"So I was opening everybody's gifts. And then I sat in front of the television—it wasn't on, but I could see my reflection on the screen—and advertised what I was opening. Well, of course, my doll, my special jointed ballerina, about eighteen or twenty inches, was my big gift, and I had opened her up when my mother walked in the door."

"When I got home, here was this mess in the living room. I had to re-wrap *everything*," Helen Kish's mother, Doris Nalty, recalled in an interview in early 2006. Looking back, Mrs. Nalty jokes that it must have been her daughter's lifelong creative streak at work: "She just couldn't resist all those pretty ribbons and paper."

Over the years, other dolls joined Helen's modest collection, with Ideal's Tiny Tears and Vogue's Ginny topping her list of favorites. But she coveted many others that the family could not afford. "My cousins Billie and Katie, Aunt Jiggie's daughters, had a cabinet chock full of Nancy Anns that were an object of fascination and envy for me throughout my childhood. I've often attributed my career as a doll artist to those unattainable little beauties," she recalls.

Helen not only collected and played with dolls, she also made paper dolls and designed their wardrobes. At age eleven, she made several dolls out of cloth.

Drawing was another passion. She recalls, "My first memory of drawing is of me in my Aunt Mai Mai's backyard. She was my godmother, and took a special interest in me from the time I was born. She often asked my mother if she could have me overnight or for a weekend. Aunt Mai Mai and Uncle Ed's home was as 'homey' to me as my own.

"I don't remember her giving me paper and pencil, but there I was in her yard, trying to draw her baby and their little dog. My godmother didn't fawn over me, but she did make it clear that she thought I had something unique and, God willing, just might amount to something."

Mrs. Nalty says, "I didn't realize that Helen was so artistic until she went to school. She would draw, and would win all of the poster contests. But I still didn't realize she was gifted; she was a good student, so I thought she was just exceptionally bright."

What Helen Kish laughingly calls her "first press clipping" dates from 1960. A large photograph in the *Rocky Mountain News* shows a beaming young Helen (along with several other children) holding her poster-size drawing of a crossing guard—one of several winners in a

Donald Nalty wears his Navy whites, circa 1942.

Donald and Doris Nalty (far left) watch the maid of honor sign their marriage license on September 4, 1948.

statewide Traffic Safety Poster Contest sponsored by the American Automobile Association.

Her main interest in drawing, however, was the human form and how to re-create it. ("I was hopeless with landscapes; never really had any desire to do them," she says.) As a result, her interest in dolls went well beyond that of most girls. She didn't just play with dolls; she studied them. "I was fascinated with how they were put together," she says. Her ballerina, with a vinyl head and a hard-plastic body, was a favorite source of study because of her poseability.

Statues and other figural art intrigued young Helen as well. While attending Sunday Mass with her family, Helen's mind would often drift from her prayer book to the church's statuary. She was so fascinated by these silent, solemn figures that while the other neighborhood kids would make snowmen, Helen tried to shape the plentiful Colorado snow into a figure that represented the Virgin Mary.

"I loved to shape things with my hands," the artist recalls. "Since snow was the only 'clean' thing I could form in my hands (my mother would have sent me packing if I had tried to dig up clay!), it was my medium."

Doris Nalty with Helen and Steve

Helen Nalty as an infant, 1950

Toddler Helen rides her tricycle in front of Grandma Mary's house in Denver.

But Art Is Not for Girls!

Without access to clay—her high school's art department didn't offer sculpting or pottery classes—Helen settled upon drawing as her creative outlet. (The interest in dolls was still there, she recalls, but since "it wasn't cool" to still like dolls in high school, Helen began to shy away from them.) She sometimes fantasized about being an artist, yet found her daydreams rudely halted by an inner voice of disbelief that scolded, "How can you do something in the arts; you're a girl!"

In the practical Nalty family, where financial resources and attention had to be divided among eight youngsters, the idea of becoming an artist was not encouraged. "This sort of thinking was dismissed. One couldn't make a living as an artist, and in any case, being a girl precluded such nonsense. Artists were always men; I didn't even know there were female artists," Helen says.

Lynn Murray, a doll collector and past president of the United Federation of Doll Clubs (UFDC), remembers this type of thinking well; she, like Helen Kish, grew up in the 1950s. Introducing the artist at a dinner function at the 2005 UFDC convention, she reminisced: "We girls had the options of helping around the house, baby-sitting, playing the clarinet in the high-school band, graduating from grade twelve and getting married. If our parents were forward-thinking, they offered us the option of becoming a nurse or a teacher so we would have 'something to fall back on' if the worst thing happened and we had to go to work."

It did occur to Helen that fashion design might be a suitable way for a girl to earn a living *and* work in art. To this end, she assembled a portfolio of drawings and sent

The artist considered her beloved Aunt Mai Mai and Uncle Ed her "second parents."

Helen at age seven proudly wears her paper and shoestring necklace (a gift from a cousin).

An early press clipping: as a youngster in 1960, Helen (far left) drew a prize-winning poster for an AAA contest; clipping from the *Rocky Mountain News.*

Contest winners—Cash prizes in either the state or the national AAA Traffic Safety Poster Contest have been awarded to each of these students, all from Denver. Left to right, the winning students, their schools and the awards are as follows: Helen Nalty, Denison School, national Second; Patricia Hatch, Denison School, state First; Connie Vaughn, West High, state First; Sally Mills, Denison School, national First; and Kathy Deuts, Morey Junior High, state First.

Rocky Mountain Motorist Photo

it to the prestigious Fashion Institute of Technology (FIT) in New York City. Her application–which included a request for financial aid (the only way she could have afforded to attend the school)—was rejected. "That was just the end of that," she recalls. "I thought, 'forget it; I'm obviously not meant to do that.'"

After the FIT rejection, Helen had no further plans for college; a decent-paying job seemed her only hope. An opportunity arose, however, with the help of a cousin. Throughout high school, Helen had worked as a baby-sitter for one of Aunt Mai Mai's daughters-in-laws, Jane. Helen and Jane often found time to talk, and the young girl told the young woman of her dreams and longings. Eager to help her bright young cousin get a college education, Jane researched on her behalf and found a school—the National College of Education in Evanston, Illinois—that would offer Helen a full scholarship.

After a year of undergraduate work, however, Helen was sure that teaching was not for her. "I didn't think it was something I would be good at, lacking the passion for it as I did," she recalls.

Determined to continue her college studies, she applied for a grant, student loans and a work/study program. With this support in place (along with a loan from a helpful uncle, Lawrence Tierney), she was able to transfer to the University of Colorado at Boulder as an art major.

Again she encountered disappointment: she soon discovered that it was difficult to get into art classes—even if you were an art major—because demand for them was so high. "And when you did get in, you didn't learn much," she says.

"This was in the late 1960s, and a lot was going on on campus," Helen recalled in a 1987 interview with me for *Dolls* magazine. "The two art professors I can remember were hippies. They were into doing their own thing, and having you do your own thing. They'd come into class the first week and give assignments, and you'd never see them again. I did get some interesting assignments, but what I really needed at the time was technical information."

After completing her sophomore year at the university, Helen traveled east to spend the summer of 1970 with her older brother, Steve, in New York City. Toying with the idea of somehow breaking into the graphics art field, she came to New York with ten dollars in her pocket and no definite plans. She left the city a short time later with the man who would soon become her husband.

Helen in prom night attire, with Grandma Mary, in 1967

Helen's high school graduation portrait, 1968

Romance and the City

In New York, Helen found employment as a switchboard operator for Abercrombie and Fitch. ("I know I got the job because I could pronounce the name," she jokes.) Brother Steve, meanwhile, had landed a summer job on Wall Street. He introduced Helen to a co-worker, who asked her for a date but then stood her up. Sensitive to his sister's bruised heart, Steve and a girlfriend took Helen along on their date to the Electric Circus discotheque in Greenwich Village—where she met her future husband, Tamas Kiss. (Tamas changed the spelling of his last name to Kish when he became a US citizen.)

"My first impression of Tamas as he approached me and gestured for me to join him on the dance floor under the spinning, mirrored disco ball was that he was stoned. He just didn't look like most guys and he didn't even try to talk to me; I soon found out why," Helen Kish recalls.

Born in Budapest, Hungary, in 1946, Tamas jokes that he left Europe for New York City in 1970 to "experience music first hand; I was a great fan of Jimmy Hendrix."

In reality, he and a friend, who was Jewish, stole away from Hungary about six months before he met Helen and found safety in a refugee camp for Jews in Italy. There they received permission to enter the United States, where they took up residence in Brooklyn. Trained as a tool and die maker, Tamas had to settle for working as a machine operator in a plastic bag factory because of his difficulty speaking the English language.

"Honestly, I don't know when exactly I feel in love with Helen, but I am sure it didn't take long," recalls Tamas. "I always had a great appreciation for beautiful women, especially because I never had the chance to be with one. I guess I got lucky for once. As soon as I met Helen, I forgot about Jimmy Hendrix."

Helen muses, "I don't recall having an idea of what 'the man of my dreams' would be like. In fact, I don't recall having any confidence that there was *any* kind of man in my future. But the funny thing is, in the year prior to meeting Tamas, I had a dream in which I was married to a man with a funny, one-syllable last name. In this dream, he was walking away from me to board a plane; I only saw him from the back. But it was him; I'm pretty sure about that."

The two soon fell in love. Shortly before Christmas, Helen returned to Colorado with Tamas. On February 13, 1971, the couple were married. The newlyweds rented an apartment in Denver and found employment, Tamas as a tool and die maker, and Helen as a switchboard operator. She still hoped to work in the arts, however, and both her dad and Tamas encouraged her to return to school.

"I had always loved all the arts, and it made me very proud to have someone with such a great talent," Tamas says. "Helen made a rag doll for me a few months after we met. I used to carry it with me, and looking at it made me feel special."

A Brush With Art

College was too costly, but night school was not. Helen enrolled at the Rocky Mountain School of Art in Denver

Tamas in New York City, 1970

Helen and Tamas in New York City, 1970

(later renamed the Rocky Mountain School of Art and Design), where she studied basics such as color theory, anatomy and life drawing (one of her favorite classes). When Helen was laid off from her job, she began attending school full-time, absorbing with relish all the information that was presented to her. "I didn't really know what I wanted to do; I just hoped I'd get into something related to art—that lighting would strike—and it did," she says.

First came a setback: financial pressures on the young couple forced Helen to leave school. She took a job as a receptionist in a photography studio, expecting the position to provide nothing but the needed paycheck. Among the services that the studio offered was the repair and restoration of old photographs. The work was handled by a freelance airbrush artist who, Helen recalls, would regularly miss deadlines.

Sensing an opportunity, Helen offered to take over the airbrushing work. "I never have been a forward person, so I don't know how I found the nerve," she recalls with a laugh.

What's more, Helen did not even know what an airbrush looked like, never mind how to use one! She phoned the director of the Rocky Mountain School of Art and asked for help. The director put her in touch with a commercial artist who willingly showed her the basics of airbrushing technique. She purchased the necessary supplies, practiced daily in the couple's apartment and soon had samples to show her boss. From that point on, she did all the airbrushing work for that studio.

Not only did the airbrushing work give Helen a start in commercial art, it also proved practical: After the birth of the couple's first child (son Tomi in 1975), she was able to continue her work on a part-time basis, first for her employer, and later, when the studio closed, for local photographers.

Adventures in Dollmaking

Before the birth of her first child, Helen made one foray into dollmaking. While working as a switchboard operator in downtown Denver, she often browsed in a small antiques shop near her office. There she found some Nancy Ann Storybook dolls—one of the many kinds of dolls she loved as a child. Fired up, she purchased a package of synthetic clay and created about twenty little dolls of children, which she gave away as gifts.

"I didn't make many, and it's a good thing, because they were awful," the artist told me in the 1987 interview for *Dolls* magazine. Ignorant of dollmaking techniques, Helen soon discovered, to her chagrin, that her dolls, which were probably not cured long enough in the oven, turned sticky. (The artist's mother still treasures her "sticky doll"—a clown—and displays it every Christmas.)

After Tomi was born, the young mother began looking for a fruitful and fun activity to fill the lonely evening hours, while baby was sleeping and Tamas attending night school. (It took thirteen years, but Tamas earned his Bachelor of Science degree and, later, a master's degree in international business.) Once again, a chance occurrence sent Helen Kish on her creative path. While shop-

Helen and Tamas Kish on their wedding day, February 13, 1971

ping in a mall, she came across a display of crafts made by local artisans. There she spied a table "full of frilly dolls." The artist remembers, "I didn't know much about antique dolls, yet I figured they weren't antiques, because the prices were too low."

Intrigued, Helen asked the seller about her wares. The woman, Ruth Nett, explained that she had made the dolls, which were porcelain. Nett then mentioned that she taught dollmaking classes in her home and asked if Helen wanted to participate. Helen couldn't believe her good fortune: at last, she would learn how to make dolls—and not the sticky kind.

The classes were not, however, what Helen had imagined. When she first arrived at her teacher's home, she was led to a table filled with greenware—unfired porcelain—and told to choose the head that she wanted to work on that day. Nett, it turned out, did not sculpt dolls; like many novice dollmakers of the mid-1970s, she would purchase commercial molds of doll heads and limbs, pour the pieces in porcelain and then assemble, paint and costume the dolls.

Though disappointed, Helen did learn how to work with greenware and porcelain. Perhaps equally as impor-

tant, Nett introduced her to the hobby of doll collecting. She told Helen about her local doll club and about the UFDC, an education-based, international organization for collectors that sponsors an annual convention and myriad regional events year-round. Now Helen knew that there were thousands of grownups who loved dolls, and were eager to buy them.

More determined than ever to make her own dolls, Helen purchased the necessary supplies, including a kiln. She researched through book after book until she found some information—"about one paragraph," she

One of Helen's infamous "sticky" dolls, circa 1974

With the Kiss family in Hungary in 1971: Helen, in the striped shirt, is flanked by Tamas's parents.

jokes—that explained how to make a plaster mold out of a sculpted clay piece. (Books on dollmaking were hard to find in the 1970s.)

"I got some plaster and got started," she recalled in the 1987 interview. "It was a disaster for about one year. There was plaster everywhere—down the pipes, on the walls. Looking back, I don't know how we lived through it."

Plaster disaster aside, Helen had, almost without realizing it, become a maker of original dolls—and in less than a year's time. She completed Aimée, her first all-porcelain, original doll, in 1975, the year of Tomi's birth. Her early efforts may have looked like a disappointing blind date—in her own words, they were "flat-faced, poorly proportioned, and badly dressed," yet they came from her own mind and hands.

The young artist's skills improved steadily, and soon her porcelain creations were receiving recognition. Helen entered some of her work in competitions (she was interviewed on local TV, baby Tomi on her hip, after winning an award at a Salvation Army Doll Tea) and sold a number of dolls through her local doll club. An upscale gift shop in Denver also began to regularly sell her work. (Tamas had convinced the shopkeeper, who had never carried dolls before, to give his wife's work a chance.)

One of the qualities that set Helen Kish's early work apart from many other porcelain dolls of the 1970s was their handpainted eyes. Typically, artists would insert purchased glass eyes into their dolls. But for Helen, these eyes were not artistically satisfying. "I just was not able to get the look that I wanted from glass eyes. Painting the eyes gave me the chance to imbue the doll's expression with more life," she says. Most of her early dolls, including Aimée, Tomi (1977) and Mary Cassatt (1978), had painted eyes.

In 1978, less than three years after making her first doll, Helen Kish was accepted as a member of the Original Doll Artists Council of America (ODACA), a peer-reviewed group of doll artists. A look at some of her dolls from this era reveals some typical-looking toddlers—cute creations, to be sure, but devoid of any distinctive personality—along with work suggestive of the successful and influential artist she would become over the next decade.

Tomi, her porcelain portrait of her son at two years old, has a sweet, soft expression that glows with the openness of early childhood. (The piece is also a spot-on likeness

The Nalty clan poses for a family portrait in 1974; Helen is in the second row, second from left.

An example of Helen Kish's airbrushed photo restoration work, circa 1975

of the fair-haired toddler.) The portrait of Tomi was made in 1977; the following year, Helen sculpted one of her first dolls to depict an adult. It was a likeness of Mary Cassatt as an elderly woman, inspired by a photograph in a biography of the artist. Like Tomi, the Cassatt portrait showed the artist's emerging ability to infuse her pieces with realism.

There were disappointments as well. Sculpting children came naturally to Helen, but sculpting babies, despite her love for them, did not. ("It's hard to have a good sense of what is going on inside them," she once mused.) She sculpted one of her first baby dolls, which she named Molly, in 1977, while pregnant with her second child. (Son Ryan was born in March of that year.) From the start, Molly was trouble. Previously, Helen had made cloth bodies for most of her dolls; this time, she decided to make a body out of composition, which, like porcelain, is poured into a mold.

"While casting it, I nearly fainted from the fumes," the artist recalls. She had planned to make a large edition of Molly, but instead made only two as she did not want to inhale fumes while pregnant.

Still, she liked the finished doll, and brought it to the first show at which she would be selling her work. Alas, Molly was cruelly panned: "A prominent Denver collector told me that it was the ugliest doll she had ever

Made in 1977, 18-inch Molly had a porcelain head and composition body.

Aimée, the artist's first original porcelain doll, was made in 1975. These versions of the 15-inch porcelain doll date from 1976.

seen," Helen recalls. "I was crushed at the time, but looking back, she may have been right."

Today, Molly enjoys a distinguished place in the Helen Kish Bad Doll Hall of Fame. While photographing dolls for the book, husband Tamas and graphic artist Dan James, who works with the couple on many projects, decided that Molly reminded them of the evil Chuckie doll from the film *Child's Play*. (A brand-new carrot-red wig that Helen fashioned for the doll contributed to the resemblance.) To make their point, they teased Helen by photographing the doll brandishing a knife. Since then, even the artist finds herself referring to the hapless baby as "Chuckie."

Discovering the Art of the Doll

Two events in the summer of 1978 helped shape Helen Kish's evolution as a doll artist. The first involved a family celebration: a surprise fiftieth birthday party for Don Brungardt, one of her favorite uncles. Eager to make a special gift for her uncle, the dollmaker set to work on a light-hearted porcelain portrait of him.

The doll of Uncle Don turned out to be a whimsical delight. His handpainted face (complete with a miniature version of Uncle Don's trademark pipe) was infused with joy and good humor. Because he was of German descent, Helen costumed him in lederhosen and posed him as if dancing. The doll, she recalls, "went over with a bang." Not only were family members impressed, so were collectors, who, after seeing pictures of the doll, asked if they could order one for themselves. Helen complied, and sold fifteen dolls of Uncle Don, each costumed differently.

Ironically, it was this piece—made with no expectations other than that it would be happily received by her uncle—that convinced Helen making dolls could be something more than a hobby. "After I made Uncle Don," she once said, "I started to think that this could be something serious, that I could really bring art into the dolls."

The second key event of the summer of 1978 was the annual national UFDC convention, held that year in Denver. At the convention, Helen would meet the late dollmaker Martha Armstrong-Hand, who inspired the young artist to reach for new heights in her work.

Born in Germany, Martha Armstrong-Hand apprenticed as a woodcarver at the Academy of Arts in Berlin.

Tomi Kish at age two was photographed by Tamas Kish near a mountain stream.

Helen's porcelain portrait of son Tomi, 13 ½ inches, was made in 1977.

In the late 1940s, she immigrated to the United States and settled in California. There she pursued a variety of crafts and artistic work, including sculpting figures for the popular Viewmaster toy slide reels. Eventually the gifted sculptor was hired by Mattel, where she worked for fifteen years. Armstrong-Hand modeled hundreds of designs, including Midge, Barbie's first best friend. Later, the pioneering doll artist began making her own porcelain characters, which quickly became recognized for both expert construction and lifelike detail. In 1977, she was accepted into NIADA.

At the UFDC convention, Armstrong-Hand was surrounded by admirers, all eager to see her latest dolls. Fortunately for Helen, a mutual acquaintance told the artist about her work. Intrigued, Armstrong-Hand invited the young dollmaker to her room for a visit. Helen received some helpful advice that day: one tip was not to study dolls, but rather "to study sculpture." But most important to Helen was the opportunity to spend some quiet, private time with a kind woman who had so much to share.

Helen recalls: "Martha talked about her life, coming to America and the difficulties she faced . . . all with such equanimity and grace showing in her face. I felt very honored. She shared photographs of her work before dolls, with Viewmaster. And lastly, she told me that she would be happy to offer her help, that it would be good to stay in touch. That opening on her part led to a correspondence, advice, mentorship and friendship."

The artist continues, "From that point on, it was my goal to be a better doll artist, a better sculptor and a member of NIADA." The qualities that Helen especially admired in Armstrong-Hand's dolls—and what she became determined to incorporate into her own work—were precision and a unique identity of design. "Martha's dolls exude a charming serenity and embody near-perfection in anatomy and execution. She set a very high benchmark for the rest of us," Helen says.

In 1978, the dollmaker was busy raising her two boys and was pregnant with her third child. (Daughter Annalise was born the following year.) Yet she made time to sculpt daily, determined to hone her skills and breathe more life into her dolls.

Works completed by the artist over the next several years show increased refinement and realism. The expression of Newsboy (1979), a nostalgic portrait of a barefoot entrepreneur of the 1930s, exudes youthful energy and

Made in 1978 for a birthday celebration, Uncle Don, 16 inches, helped give the artist confidence that she could take her work to new heights.

Proud Poppa Tamas Kish poses with his baby boys, Tomi and Ryan, in 1978.

eagerness. The perky paperboy helped the artist net news coverage of her own: the doll was shown on the cover of the March 1980 issue of *The Antiques Journal*.

"I saw a future for Helen in her dollmaking early on; her work always seemed to be alive and beautiful," the artist's father says. Newsboy, Mr. Nalty adds, was one of his favorite dolls: "This paper boy resembled my brother as a boy so much that it was uncanny."

Pouty (1981), a sad-faced little girl with furrowed brows, is one of the artist's early favorites, although more for technical reasons than sentimental ones: "With Pouty, I think that I achieved more grace of proportion, as well as a leap forward in my anatomy," she says.

Established doll artists soon recognized Helen Kish's talent. With dolls like Pouty, she earned her much longed-for acceptance into NIADA in 1981. "I felt like Queen for a Day," she recalls. "Learning I had been accepted into NIADA was one of the happiest days of my life, exceeded only by the birth of my children."

After her acceptance into NIADA, Helen became involved in the organization's activities. From 1985 through 1988, she served as standards chairman; her responsibilities included reviewing the work of artists applying for membership (including the dolls made by a young Robert Tonner, who has since become one of America's most successful and influential doll manufacturers). Later, from 1991 through 1994, she served two consecutive terms as the group's president.

A Decade of Dolls

From the late 1970s to the late 1980s, Helen Kish sculpted more than one hundred dolls. Collectors didn't see all of them, however. After being scrutinized by her increasingly critical eye, many pieces never left her

Helen Kish's first cover story was the March 1980 issue of *The Antiques Journal*.

The artist with some of her earliest creations, including Newsboy (back row, far left), circa 1981

studio. "I would never sell something that I felt was sculpturally inferior," she asserts.

By the early 1980s, the Kishes were settled in their second house, a roomy, two-story home in the Denver suburb of Littleton. Each of the children had their own bedroom. The dollmaker set aside a corner of the family room for pattern making, sewing and other less messy tasks. A large basement offered enough space for a wet studio, where she did all of her sculpting, casting, painting and firing. She had named her one-woman operation "Helen Kish Originals," and sold her work primarily at shows.

Most of Helen's dolls depicted youngsters, usually female. By the mid-1980s, her distinctive artistic signature had fully matured: her girls bore gently realistic expressions, usually with the pert, bee-stung lip shape that has since become one of her trademarks.

Babies and adults were becoming an increasing part of her output, however. One of the artist's favorite dolls of this period is an all-porcelain, jointed baby doll from 1993, her second doll based on son Ryan. "Ryan was a successful attempt at the kind of jointing that we all admired in Martha's work," she says. "It was more than the standard jointing at the neck, shoulders and hips; Ryan was composed of fifteen porcelain parts, jointed at the neck, ribs, shoulders, elbows, wrists, hips, knees and ankles."

But it was the artist's depictions of adults that underwent the most radical change. Her early adult figures (such as Uncle Don) had personality, yet tended toward caricature. Her adult figures of the early and mid-1980s, however, were powerful sculptures—haunting, moody and memorable—beginning with the breathtaking twenty-two-inch-tall Victoriana (1983), which graced the cover of the March/April 1988 issue of *Dolls* magazine.

With Victoriana, Helen's goal was to embody the mysterious essence of Meryl Streep's title character in the 1981 film *The French Lieutenant's Woman*. "I couldn't get that film out of my head. The images kept on haunting me. Finally, I made the doll to exorcise the images from my mind," the artist recalled in 1987.

The piece delighted everyone: artist, collectors, media, colleagues. "With Victoriana, I captured exactly what I wanted—just the right emotional response," Helen said in 1987. Collectors clamored to acquire the doll, so much so that after Helen completed the edition of fifteen, she

Ryan Kish at age two

Helen created this porcelain portrait of son Ryan, 16 inches, in 1982.

A family portrait, circa 1979

created a similar edition, Victoriana 2, to appease collectors who were not able to acquire the first version. (Victoriana 2 was smaller than her predecessor, and her face slightly different.)

Victoriana was only the third contemporary doll to be featured on a cover of *Dolls* magazine. Krystyna Poray Goddu, the publication's founding editor, recalls that when some ten years' of *Dolls* covers were hung on the walls of the magazine's art department, publisher Robert Campbell Rowe proclaimed the one featuring Victoriana "the best *Dolls* magazine cover ever."

"Victoriana caused quite a stir when she was introduced," remembers Robert Tonner. "She had such a unique look; she was also a large doll, which added to her grandness. The doll was truly spectacular."

Although not as famous as Victoriana, Diva was more dificult to sculpt. Also inspired by an actress in a film—Wihelmenia Wiggins-Fernandez in the 1981 French thriller *Diva*—the thirty-inch-high doll was created in 1984. What made this doll especially challenging was that Helen wanted her to appear to be singing, and sculpting an open mouth can result in an unappealing facial expression.

The artist's efforts were successful; Diva seems to be caught mid-song, her raised brows, wide eyes, pursed mouth and graceful, expressive hands all working together, like instruments in an orchestra, to convey a musical moment of beauty. (The doll's low-cut gown also gave the dollmaker an opportunity to sculpt an area of the body that fascinated her: the sides of the neck and the dip of the clavicle, which she had not dared explore as a less seasoned sculptor.) "I often wish I still had this doll in my own collection so that I could examine her today; she just 'happened,' as if someone else was working through me," the artist said in 2005.

Although Helen began to explore other mediums in the late 1980s, the look and feel of porcelain delighted her senses. "I think it's a beautiful medium to work with," she told me in 1987. Helen's smaller dolls typically had either all-porcelain bodies or porcelain heads, arms and legs attached with a wire armature to a cloth body. Larger pieces, such as Victoriana and Diva, often had inserts of ultra suede attached beneath the bust and reaching to the waist.

The process of turning a clay sculpture into a porcelain doll is both laborious and challenging. In an autobio-

Annalise in antique bonnet and gown cradles Girl with a Molded Cap, early 1980s.

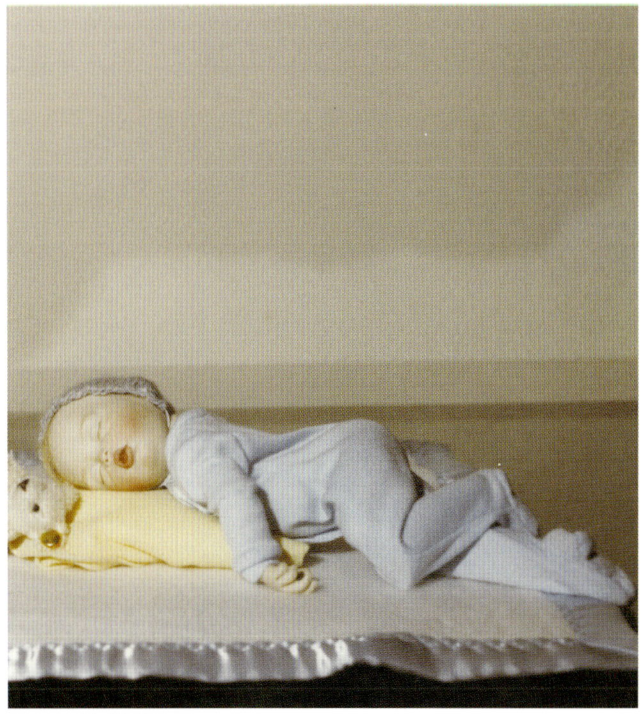

Ryan, 13 inches, 1983, was one of the artist's first porcelain dolls with multiple ball joints.

graphical essay published in *The Art of the Doll* (NIADA, 1992), Helen described the many steps involved, as well as some of her tricks of the trade:

When I work in porcelain, my initial models are sculpted in a hard oil-based clay, which is cut up into small pieces, worked and softened in the hands. After the preliminary models are finished, waste molds are made. The wax models are tooled until they are acceptable, or can be taken no further, preferably until as smooth as glass. (Begin with a fine sandpaper—say 230 grit—and gradually increase the number to 600 grit, finishing off with a polishing cloth. An alcohol burner can be useful, but is extremely tricky. Use a waxer to add to, or make significant changes in, the wax cast.)

The production molds are made over the finished wax models. Casting should not take place until the molds are thoroughly dried at room temperature.

I follow the traditional method for this part of the process, with special care to protect my lungs from porcelain dust. My studio is equipped with an industrial dust collector. All cleaning is done at this station, with mask in place.

The firing process includes the bisque fire, in which the porcelain reaches maturation, and three to five china firings, going from lights to darks. From this point, the figure is assembled, wigged and costumed. I design all of my costumes, and it is not unusual to try out several ideas before settling on one design.

Like Helen, Robert Tonner began his career making porcelain dolls. The two met in 1985 at the annual NIADA conference, held that year in New York City. Then the novice, Tonner attended the event to have his work critiqued, and Helen was one of the artists who reviewed his work. The like-minded pair soon developed a mutual admiration for each other's work that has remained steadfast for more than twenty years. (In 1998, the two even collaborated on a porcelain doll: Sophie, the souvenir for the 36th annual NIADA conference.)

"Helen has, from the start, been one of the industry's finest sculptors," Robert Tonner asserted in 2005. "The first porcelain dolls of hers that I saw had an unbelievable attention to detail, and a delicacy that few sculp-

The artist paints a porcelain head in her basement studio in the early 1980s.

Inspired by Meryl Streep's performance in *The French Lieutenant's Woman,* Victoriana was shown on the March/April 1988 cover of *Dolls.*

tors could match."

Tonner continued, "What I respond to in Helen's work is the inherent gentleness and calmness in the faces she sculpts. Realism is hard to do—you have to do it just right, or a figure can be really awkward. Helen not only knows the anatomy, but also is able to idealize without losing that realism—a very tricky thing to do."

By 1990, Helen Kish's porcelain dolls were selling from $450 to about $1,500 and up. Most of these pieces were sold at the annual NIADA convention; others were sold through select shops or through the artist via mail orders. At this point, her output fell into three categories: art pieces like Victoriana (these were either made in small editions or were one-of-a-kind); lower-priced, limited-edition children and babies; and commercial designs (discussed on the following pages). Eager for more experience, the artist had begun to sculpt in stoneware clay. She also made figures and busts in porcelain, terra-cotta and clay that she hoped to have produced in bronze.

From Maker to Manufacturer

Given the artist's skill and popularity, it is not surprising that her work caught the eye of a number of mass-market

With Diva, 1984, the artist successfully sculpted a study of an opera singer captured mid-song.

purveyors of dolls. Beginning in the early 1980s, Helen Kish was contracted to design dolls for several well-known companies. The Franklin Mint commissioned the artist to create prototypes for porcelain dolls, while R. Dakin and Company invited her to make porcelain prototypes for vinyl production. From the 1980s through the early 1990s, she also worked on designs for The Danbury Mint, the San Francisco Music Box Company and The Hamilton Collection.

Ultimately, however, Helen found commercial design disappointing. In a letter to me in October 1987, she lamented, "I am concerned about having my name associated with commercial products, because I have found that I don't have any control over the quality of the product."

The money that she was counting on for the design work—which she hoped would supplement the income from the sales of her original dolls—was never plentiful. In some cases, projects fell through, and she did not receive any payment for her efforts. Yet, the various design projects were a learning experience that would prove invaluable when Helen launched her own company for the production of vinyl dolls in 1991.

Beginning in the mid-1980s, a number of pioneering German artists either set up factories of their own, or worked with existing manufacturers, to produce vinyl dolls of high quality. Annette Himstedt's vinyl line, launched in 1986, was an instant hit, as were the beautiful vinyl dolls designed by German artists Hildegard Günzel and Rotraut Schrott and Swiss artist Sylvia Natterer. Several successful American dollmakers, most notably Julie Good-Krüger and Susan Wakeen, entered the vinyl market early on as well.

It was the vinyl dolls designed by another talented German, Sabine Esche, that inspired Helen to explore the medium herself. "I saw several dolls by Sabine Esche at a doll show," the artist recalls. "They were captivatingly beautiful portraits that looked like real children. They also looked, to me, like porcelain. When the vendor told me that they were German dolls, vinyl, I guess it just awakened my American spirit of competition, to be quite frank. I thought, 'if they can do that with vinyl, why can't we?'"

Fortuitously, Helen had recently received a large royalty check from the sales of one of her commercial designs for The Hamilton Collection. This seed money, combined with her enthusiasm, helped the artist get started on her new venture. The first thing she did was make phone calls—seemingly endless phone calls!—to find someone who could help her learn how to turn her sculptures into vinyl.

The support of her husband—which the artist had been able to count on throughout her career—was especially critical at this time. While Helen researched the manufacturing aspects of vinyl production, Tamas set up the business end, analyzing costs, marketing and distribution. In 1991, after about a year of diligent work, the couple's newest baby—christened Kish & Company (its slogan was "for The True Collector")—was born. Helen handled all design responsibilities and the dolls were produced in vinyl in the United States. To get the dolls to shops, the Kishes joined forces with European Artist Dolls, a distribution company founded by Danny and Barrie Shapiro, owners of The Toy Shoppe, a popular store for collectible dolls and bears in Midlothian, Virginia.

Before Helen Kish's first vinyls appeared, however, many mishaps had to be overcome. "There were surprises at every stage, so many bugs to work out," the artist said in an early 1991 interview. The creation of the dolls' arms was one of the hitches that held up production.

"The first set of arms—I was so proud of them!—just would *not* come out of the molds," Helen lamented. "There were too many bends—almost ninety degrees at the elbow and another bend at the wrist. I had to go back to square one and re-do them completely, changing the position of the arms."

At last, at the end of the year, Helen Kish's first vinyl dolls began to ship. Named Kelsey, Mary Kate and Margie, the dolls were part of a nostalgic collection called "Children of Yesteryear . . . When We Were Little Girls." Each doll had the same face, but the trio were costumed, wigged and painted differently. Each girl symbolized a generation. Margie, with her bobbed hair and soft-white, drop-waist dress, represented the 1930s. The pig-tailed Mary Kate, garbed in a plaid dress and saddle shoes, was reminiscent of the 1950s. And blonde-haired Kelsey, wearing a floral mini dress, represented the 1970s. Kelsey, Mary Kate and Margie stood ten and one-half inches high and were limited to an edition of 1,500 apiece; each retailed for $195.

Like Helen Kish's handmade porcelain dolls, the vinyl girls were realistic in their look and refined in their execution. Facial expressions were augmented by crevices around the nose and mouth; fingers, which had been individually sculpted, were long and graceful. Helen spared no expense on the details: the dolls' wigs were crafted of human hair; shoes were made of ultra leather; and each doll was painted by hand—by the artist herself.

Tomi, Annalise and Ryan in front of the Kish home, circa 1982

Shelves in the artist's basement studio house heads for original dolls as well as commercial designs.

The latter was not Helen's plan; she had hoped to train artisans to paint the dolls to her satisfaction. But she was unable to find suitable helpers, and so took on the work herself. It was laborious, yet painting the dolls did ensure the one thing she was most concerned about: complete control over the result. "If, at any point, these dolls are not what I want them to be, I want to drop this," she confided to me in 1991.

There was no need for the artist to worry. From the start, the new dolls were greeted with enthusiasm. "It was with great trepidation that we sent Kelsey, Mary Kate and Margie off to the 1991 Toy Fair," the artist says. "But at the end of the first day of the show, we got a call from Danny and Barrie: They told us to open a bottle of champagne, that our little girls were a huge success!"

"I think Helen stunned the art-doll world when she introduced her vinyl dolls," Robert Tonner observed in an interview in 2006. "And I saw more than an artist applying her art to what was previously viewed as a 'commercial' medium: I saw the future! At the time, I remember thinking that what Helen was doing was creating the doll company of the future. And, it turns out I was right. Those first

dolls of hers hold up today as super works—the vinyl play doll as art!"

Not surprisingly, the dolls received heavy coverage in *Dolls* magazine and other publications for collectors. What's more, Kelsey was nominated for a *Dolls* Awards of Excellence—the first of many nominations that Helen would receive for her vinyl dolls.

Before the release of the Kish & Company vinyl dolls, collector Tim Purk of Rye Brook, New York, was familiar with the artist's work. He still remembers the day he saw the vinyl doll Meggie, one of Helen's designs for Dakin, in a shopping mall in White Plains, New York. "Meggie's face was different from any of the other dolls in the shop, and I like dolls that are special and different," Purk recalls. Several years later, when the Children of Yesteryear debuted, he decided it was time to add Helen Kish's work to his collection of contemporary dolls.

"I saw Margie in a doll shop and was taken with the simplicity of design and the period portrayed," the collector says. "I also liked the fact that she could be safely handled and 'played with.'"

Helen Kish says, "Aside from the Shapiros calling us from

The 1991 brochure for the debut vinyl collection from Kish & Company

Master vinyl head for Mary Kate, handpainted and wigged

the New York Toy Fair to tell us to pop the cork on the champagne, we knew very little about the public response until the dolls shipped and letters began to come in from collectors. They trickled in at first, but they were always wonderfully positive. Often a letter would arrive on the very day that I needed encouragement the most."

The Vinyl Venture Continues

It was a while before Helen Kish would find time to design new dolls and expand her line, but in 1993 she added three characters—Sugar, Hannah and Andie—to the Children of Yesteryear collection. Like their predecessors, the dolls were limited to 1,500, and they were still handpainted by the artist. (The charming trio were shown on the cover of the September 1993 issue of *Contemporary Doll Magazine*.)

Later that same year, there was a key change in the Kish & Company line: with encouragement from the Shapiros and European Artist Dolls, production was moved overseas to a factory in Spain. Helen continued to design the dolls and their costumes, but the factory did the rest—including painting the dolls.

With her responsibilities lessened, the artist was able to focus more on sculpting and designing. In 1994 Kish & Company released the All Dressed Up collection, which debuted with four characters (Aimee Lin, Jesse, Kristina and Michaela). The artist's first jointed vinyl dolls, the twelve-and-a-half-inch pieces were articulated at the neck, shoulders, elbows, hips and knees. In June of that year, Helen traveled to Spain to approve the final production dolls. "I was a little worried about the jointing, because it was new," she said in a 1994 interview. "But the company came up with a unique system completely on their own. They developed a very hard plastic joint, which works beautifully. I was enraptured with what they had done; they just did a fabulous job."

Over the next several years, the vinyl line would more than double in size. In 1995, the artist introduced her Childhood Favorites collection, a series of jointed vinyl dolls that celebrated beloved characters from fairy tales, children's stories and nursery rhymes. The collection debuted with The Little Match Girl, the tragic title character of an 1846 Hans Christian Andersen story. She was an unusual and daring choice; one would expect a collection of fairy tale-inspired dolls to launch with a happily-ever-after heroine such as Red Riding Hood or Cinderella. In contrast, the impoverished, barefoot match-seller of Andersen's tale "looked the picture of misery," and dies of cold and starvation.

"It is quite a sad story with a heart-breaking conclusion," Helen admits, "but it was one of my favorite Hans Christian Andersen tales and I very much wanted to try to bring her to life."

Perhaps misery, indeed, loves company, for the sad-faced Little Match Girl was a success, winning a *Dolls* Award of Excellence that year. "The Little Match Girl was poignant and beautiful at the same time—and Helen was able to sell a doll without shoes!" marvels Robert Tonner. "Helen never takes the iconic look of a character. She is able to make it her own, which is one of the qualities that sets her apart from other doll designers," he adds.

East Coast collector Judy Rosenbaum treasures her small, apartment-friendly collection of Kish & Company dolls, which began with Penny from the 1995 Dance! and Play collection and Lynne (also known as Lynee) from the 1996 Ballerinas group. "My little Lynne, with her rosebud mouth, was my first Kish doll," she says. "The beautiful workmanship of the doll—she balances so well that she stands on her own—and the subtle, expressive modeling and painting of her face still stand out for me."

Cowgirl Penny has a very different expression from most of Helen Kish's little girls: her mouth is narrow, wide and smiling, rather than pert and pursed. "She is such a kidlike doll that she always coaxes a smile from me," Rosenbaum says. "Her face is one of the best, most natu-

Helen Kish's first vinyl dolls to be featured on a magazine cover were Sugar, Hannah and Andie on the September 1993 issue of *Contemporary Doll Magazine*.

ral child faces I have ever encountered on a doll, with a gently conspiratorial smile that makes her look as though she's just thought of a joke. Even her eyes smile!"

In 1996 and 1997, Helen introduced vinyl dolls based on more of her favorite themes, including the ballerinas, siblings and characters based on famous paintings. In 1997, she debuted her first vinyl baby dolls, Carolyn and Elizabeth. A new twelve-inch body was used in the Kish & Company line that year, as was a warmer dark skin tone for black dolls like the sweet-faced siblings Naomi and Tooloo.

Paula Reding, co-owner (with daughters Shannon McQueen and Kaley Haavind) of the Denver Doll Emporium, began carrying Kish dolls in her shop in the mid-1990s, beginning with the ballerinas, the baby dolls and The Wizard of Oz collection from the Childhood Favorites group. "I remember being impressed with the dolls' delicate hands, sensitive, charming faces and the wonderful painted eyes—and of course what really stands out in Helen's work are those beautifully shaped and shaded lips!" Reding says.

The Anne of Green Gables doll, added to the

Helen's poignant interpretation of Hans Christian Andersen's Little Match Girl was made in 1995.

Childhood Favorites collection in 1997, caught the eye of Marianne McGarrity, a New Jersey-based collector. "I loved her serious face, and I had loved the book, so I bought her," McGarrity recalls.

That one doll was the beginning of a love affair with Kish's work. By 2005, McGarrity owned more than fifty of the artist's dolls; she also regularly pens articles for the Kish Collectors' Society newsletter. "Helen is a true sculptor," she says. "The bodies and hands and attention to detail in her work still amaze me; even the feet are arched and detailed realistically. The faces are expressive and soulful; there is nothing 'cookie cutter cute' about them."

The vinyl line continued to expand in 1998 with the addition of more than twenty new dolls. In 1999, Helen debuted her first vinyl adult character, the statuesque Isabelle Rose. In her debut appearance, Isabelle Rose was costumed in a late-nineteenth-century-style frock with leg-o'-mutton sleeves. With her dreamy yet intelligent expression, the beautiful doll looked as if she just stepped out of the pages of a romance novel. A winner of a *Dolls* Award of Excellence that year, Isabelle Rose, at twenty-eight inches, was Helen Kish's tallest vinyl creation to date.

From 1991 through 1996, Helen designed all the costumes for her vinyl line. In 1997, she was introduced to the German-born clothing designer Rosemarie Ionker. Helen and Ionker collaborated on several costumes in the 1997 and 1998 lines. For the next two years, the artist turned more of the clothing design over to Ionker, who would develop the costumes based on the dollmaker's sketches.

With the artist's responsibilities for Kish & Company decreasing, she was able to find more time to devote to other long-neglected projects. In 1994, she was delighted with her newly emerging free time: "I really see it starting to open up now, which is great. I'm doing quite a lot of modeling. It makes me happy, I tell you!" she confided then.

By the late 1990s, however, the artist began to feel differently about her role in Kish & Company, as well as some of the directions the company was taking. But in the meantime, she exuberantly devoted her time to creating porcelain dolls as well as pieces in stoneware and bronze.

Introducing Helen Cunalta Kish

The myriad tasks involved in getting a new company up and running, combined with her responsibilities as the president of NIADA (her terms ran from 1991 through 1994), prevented Helen from creating many sculptures in porcelain. Yet she tried whenever she could to give herself the increasing luxury of devoting many hours to the creation of a one-of-a-kind or strictly limited-edition doll.

Oftentimes, she found that a strong emotional response to an event or the reading of a powerful poem would inspire her to retreat to the solace of her studio and her clay. In 1991, distraught because of the death of blues guitarist Stevie Ray Vaughn in a helicopter crash, Helen sculpted a one-of-a-kind portrait doll of the artist whose music and performances she had followed for years. "Nothing has ever hit me like this hit me," she told me in 1991. She modeled the portrait in porcelain clay, a medium to which she had become increasingly drawn.

"Working in direct-modeling porcelain, not cast porcelain, is really challenging," the artist said in late 1993. "It's tough stuff to work with. It dries very quickly, and if you don't have every single piece of the entire sculpture drying at exactly the same time, it is likely to crack."

In late 1987, when Helen was interviewed for a cover story in *Dolls*, she expressed a need to try some new projects, craving what she called "the freedom to do more off-the-wall things with my originals." In 1993, she did just that. At the NIADA conference, held that year in Chicago, she unveiled La Llorona, an emotionally charged figure sculpted directly in porcelain clay.

The piece was inspired by a widespread Mexican-American legend that has numerous variations and is known from South America to southwestern America.

At the heart of every version, however, is a "weeping woman" who drowns her children in despair over a faithless lover. Helen's compelling twenty-five-inch figure of the suffering woman showed intense anguish and pain, which surprised many collectors of her work. She recalls: "At the NIADA show, I overheard one woman say, 'You know, I love her work, but I don't understand *this*.'"

In the early 1990s, Helen also began to experiment with stoneware clay. "I love the feel of it; I love the texture," she said at the 1994 debut of The Sentinel, one of her earliest stoneware pieces, at the annual NIADA conference.

The 1990s also saw the debut of Helen's first bronze pieces, which she had longed to produce for a number of years. Her creations in this medium have included dainty winged angels, busts and dramatic adult figures such as The Turn, a male figure inspired by a modern-day interpretation of the epic poem *Beowulf*.

At art doll shows in the late 1990s, Helen would often display her latest bronze creations alongside her better-known porcelain ones. In 1999, at the fourth annual show organized by Janet Marchese, then owner of The Angel Keeper shop, the artist showed her polar-opposite artistic

Nannette (1995) sans costume shows the jointing system designed for the Kish & Company 12 ½-inch vinyl dolls.

Cowgirl Penny, 1995, lassoed collectors' hearts with her twinkling eyes and broad smile.

sides with angel-themed works in both mediums. Winged Veronica, an adorable and playful baby angel, was made of porcelain; Guardian of Little Angels, a solemn maternal angel with three young charges, was a bas-relief cast in bronze. (The latter piece, which made a dramatic statement, was featured on the event invitation.)

Working in bronze not only gave the artist the chance to spread her creative wings, but also offered the opportunity to add to her formal art education. In the summers of 1996 and 1997, she took intensive, week-long sculpting seminars with Bruno Lucchesi, an Italian-born artist renowned for his work in bronze. His pieces are in the permanent collections of many major American museums, including the Metropolitan Museum of Art and Whitney Museum in New York City, and his work is the subject of four books (including *Modeling the Figure in Clay* and *Modeling the Head in Clay*; Watson Guptill Publications, 1996), some of which he authored and some that he illustrated. In her home studio, Helen Kish studied and poured over the Lucchesi books countless times, savoring every nuance of the sculptor's masterful figurative work. When she learned that he would be

teaching at the Loveland Academy of Fine Arts in Loveland, Colorado, she was overjoyed.

"Being in the same studio with Bruno Lucchesi was almost an out-of-body experience for me," the dollmaker recalls. "To say that I was, and still am, in awe doesn't quite describe it. Watching him work was, to me, like watching a miracle happen. Did the experience change or affect my work? It's hard for me to say. But it isn't often one has the chance to be in the presence of greatness and humility all wrapped up in one man. Maestro Lucchesi is such a man."

To differentiate her stoneware and bronze pieces from her popularly known porcelain and vinyl dolls, she adopted a new artistic signature: Helen Cunalta Kish. (Cunalta is the pre-Anglicized version of Nalty, her maiden name.) In a brochure produced by the Kishes in the late 1990s, the artist noted that her creative path to becoming a dollmaker had returned her to the realization she had experienced in childhood: that to sculpt—even in the snow—was one of her greatest joys. She wrote:

"This circuitous route has brought me back to that early revelation and with it the rapture in giving over to the spiritual, sublime and primal process of finding form in clay, of uncovering the eternal in the finite."

Even these varied experiments did not fully quench the artist's thirst to create. Beginning in the 1980s, Helen had made jewelry whenever she craved a break from figural art. She continued to craft one-of-a-kind jewelry, using imaginative blends of semi-precious stones, throughout the 1990s (and continues to do so). During that decade, she also experimented freely with busts, bas-reliefs and figurines in a variety of mediums, including clay, terra-cotta and resin. Many of these pieces were given away as gifts, and are consequently rarely seen.

In an interview with writer Kathleen Ryan for the February/March 1999 issue of *Contemporary Doll Collector*, Helen cheerfully acknowledged the continued broadening of her artistic wings: "I've been all over the map with my art, and it's one of the things that drives people crazy about me. I keep moving around and challenging myself because art is my passion—I go wherever it leads me."

With her dreamy expression, beautiful Isabelle Rose (1999) looks like a heroine from a romantic novel.

The Best of All Worlds

In the late 1990s, it appeared that Helen Kish had the best of both worlds. She had a thriving vinyl business, and was able to produce her own small editions and one-of-a-kind works of art. But, behind the scenes, dissatisfaction loomed. Since the early 1990s, the dollmaker had accepted an increasingly smaller role in the business end of Kish & Company. While this gave her more time for creative ventures, she and husband Tamas came to feel, by 1997, that they needed to take full control of the direction of the Kish & Company line.

"Danny and Barrie Shapiro were pivotal in the early years of Kish & Company because they had the marketing know-how that we lacked. And their enthusiasm for our dolls was contagious," the artist says. "In time, though, it became clear that European Artist Dolls and our production company in Spain had one goal, and we had another."

Citing creative differences as the impetus for the split from European Artist Dolls, the artist and her husband—who was now working with Helen full-time—represented the Kish & Company line in their own booth at the 1998 Toy Fair. "At Toy Fair, European Artist Dolls had a full line of Kish & Company dolls that I had designed, and we showed a completely separate line of vinyls with a new sculpt—Pippi—and a number of limited-edition porcelains," the dollmaker says.

On the surface, it may have appeared to collectors that nothing had changed. Helen Kish was still producing delightful dolls, garnering awards and magazine covers from the leading doll publications. (Isabelle Rose won a 1999 *Dolls* Award of Excellence; that same year, baby doll Marisa earned a *Doll Reader* DOTY Award.) But it was no easy task for the artist and her husband to tackle the myriad responsibilities of running a business.

"It was actually my idea that Tamas come into the business; the time was right and our skills were complementary. We felt we could learn the rest," Helen says. "But our learning curve swallowed up Tamas's retirement fund and cost us our home. But one thing we have in common is tenacity. It got us through, and has kept us going. We don't waste time regretting the past, there is too much to be accomplished in the present."

At first, the couple continued to have the dolls produced in Spain. When this arrangement failed, Kish & Company switched to a US-based production, which also did not work to the Kishes' satisfaction, and so by 2003, they switched production of the dolls to a factory in China.

At the 1999 doll show sponsored by The Angel Keeper, Helen holds her petite porcelain angel, Winged Veronica.

Problems and pitfalls aside, Helen moved forward with recasting the direction of her vinyl line. In 2000, she divided her offerings into two categories: the high-end, Signature Edition line and the lower-priced LadyKish line. ("LadyKish" was a pet moniker once given to the artist by fitness guru Richard Simmons, an enthusiastic collector.) The Signature Editions were conceived as sophisticated pieces that would be sold in small editions (typically 75 to 200) and handpainted by Helen herself. In 2000, the Signature Editions retailed for about $400 and up and included elegant pieces like the ballerina Coppelia.

In contrast, the LadyKish dolls were designed and aimed for a broader collector market. They were either unlimited or sold in large editions (usually 300 and up) and, in 2000, sold for about $170 to $220. The debut LadyKish line included twelve-inch Bethany and sixteen-inch Jo, which quickly found their way into collectors' hearts. "The Bethany and Jo sculpts are huge favorites with my customers," noted Denver Doll Emporium co-owner Paula Reding in 2006.

Not only was the 2000 line well received (Coppelia and Bethany were nominated for *Dolls* Awards of Excellence, and Bethany won a 2000 *Doll Reader* DOTY Award), but the Kishes also soon received an unexpected, yet most timely, boon. It came in late 2000, via a fax from Pleasant Company, maker of the American Girls Collection of historically themed dolls and books. In an unpublished interview with Krystyna Poray Goddu, the artist recalled the day that Tamas burst into her workroom, where she was assembling dolls, waving a fax:

"I saw the Pleasant Company logo and grabbed it. They were looking for sculptors and was I interested? I had Tamas call them right away, saying yes, we're interested, and it went from there. I never prayed so hard for anything, because I was not the only sculptor in the running for the project. I wanted this more than I had wanted anything for a long, long time."

The project under development was a collection of vinyl dolls (accompanied, as are all the company's dolls, by books) with an international theme, called Girls of Many Lands. "Everything about it seemed right for me," the artist continued. "As a person who loves books and would probably spend her last dollar on books—and who believes so much in giving girls power through education—I felt the project was a perfect fit."

The artist's instincts proved correct: Helen Kish and Pleasant Company fit together as smoothly as Cinderella and her glass slipper. "Working with the creative team

Helen Kish with award-winning sculptor Bruno Lucchesi, circa 1997

A one-of-a-kind jewelry suite made by the artist in 2000 combined amethyst, ametrine and freshwater pearls with her own sculpted fairies, cast in resin.

from the Pleasant Company was the pinnacle of my experience in commercial design," the artist asserts. "Not only was the process challenging and the exchanges between their team and ours respectful and productive, but the end product was really exceptional."

For the Girls of Many Lands (GOML) project, Helen first sketched, then sculpted, five faces of children to represent nations from around the world, including England, China and India. (A year later, she created an additional sculpt for the collection, which was used for the Ethiopian girl.) "The identity of each girl was determined by the GOML team, and it was left to me to come up with a look that would represent a girl from that ethnic group," the artist says.

Helen also sculpted the body shared by each of the dolls, experimenting with various sizes before Pleasant Company chose a final height of nine inches. Garbed in detailed, colorful garments designed by Pleasant Company's creative team ("they put a lot of effort into the accuracy of the costumes," the artist says), the Girls of Many Lands were released in 2002 and 2003. As is typical for Pleasant Company, the dolls were not marketed under their sculptor's name. However, Helen was credited in

Coppelia, one of the artist's Signature Editions, was released in 2000.

company press releases; she was also asked to inscribe her signature on the doll body: it appears on the bottom of the left foot.

"All of the dolls in this collection had Helen's trademark rosebud mouth and were delectable," says collector Judy Rosenbaum. "I snapped up the Turkish one, Leyla, who is dressed in an astonishingly delicate tissue-weight silk. Leyla has an interesting face that is reminiscent of Persian illuminated manuscripts."

The new century ushered in more happy developments for the Kishes. In 2000, the Kish Collectors' Society, a club for dedicated fans, was born. Daughter Annalise Kish began working with her parents in 2002, helping with various administrative duties and taking charge of the Kish Collectors' Society. "I have always been very proud of my mother's work," she says. And, in 2003, the Kishes moved into their new home in downtown Denver.

The Kishes had lost their home in the Denver suburbs after taking full control of Kish & Company. Helen recalls: "We had moved the business out of our home and into a commercial space at a time when we thought we had investors. The investors fell through, and expenses mounted. We sold our house to avoid foreclosure, and moved into an apartment, which I hated, and then to another. At the time, I thought we would never own a home again."

In time, however, they located a run-down but ideal spot in which to live and work: a corner brick building in Denver, zoned for both commercial and residential occupancy, which Helen jokingly calls "our very own broke-down palace."

The building has a charming pedigree. Built in 1912 by Emilio Varone, an Italian immigrant (this area of downtown Denver was known as "Little Italy" at one time), it housed a grocery downstairs and living quarters for the Varone family upstairs. Now the Kishes and their dog live on the top floor. The downstairs storefront, expanded by Varone in the 1920s, houses the artist's studio and Annalise's work area.

It is indeed a family affair at 33rd Avenue in downtown Denver. Tom, the Kishes' eldest son, lives down the street, and stops by regularly, often accompanied by his pet dog, who joyfully visits with the Kishes' dog, Morphy (a black Lab mix) and Annalise's beagle, Carlo (the model for Riley's pet dog, Jingles). Annalise's home, a tidy cottage, is just three blocks away. Son Ryan, who works as an information technologist administrator, resides in Denver, and moonlights as "the IT guy" for Kish & Company. Helen's sister, Anne, lives in the metro area as well, and she and the artist see each other frequently.

When all the Kish canines bark simultaneously, it can become "far too noisy to do business on the telephone," the artist admits cheerfully (company employee Kassem

Hab Hab brings his beagle, Buddah, to the office as well!). But noise aside, the closeness of the Kish family often brings levity to the pressures of work—a buoyancy that characterizes the most successful doll released by the artist at the beginning of the twenty-first century.

Riley, Electra and the Fashion Doll Phenomenon

In 2003, Helen Kish released two dolls that became collectors' favorites, and a third that quickly became their obsession. The first of the terrific troika was Bitty Bethany. In 2000, Helen had introduced Bethany, a twelve-inch vinyl cutie-pie with a wide-eyed, "love me" look. Bethany appealed not only to the traditional, longtime Kish collector who appreciates a doll mainly for aesthetic appeal, but also to the growing number of collectors who enjoy interacting with, and sewing for, their dolls. In 2003, the artist released the popular Bethany in a more compact—and less costly—eleven-inch size, appropriately named Bitty Bethany. (That same year, she changed the name of the LadyKish line to the LadyKish Whimsies, partly to reflect Bethany's new size.)

The next fabulous face was that of the statuesque Electra. Helen's third vinyl lady, sixteen-inch Electra debuted as the convention souvenir at the 2003 Modern Doll Collectors Convention, wearing a white gown and an elaborate, shimmering headdress. In 2004, the artist added the doll to her LadyKish Whimsies line. "I wanted an adult figure in the line for all the design possibilities that go with dressing an adult," she says. "I also wanted to position her as an ethereal character—a shape-shifter or time traveler (a kind of 'Orlando'), rather than have her compete in the contemporary fashion doll world."

In 2004, stately Electra was joined by her "spirit sister," Rio, in the Facets of the Eternal Feminine collection. The characters have appeared in a number of glamorous guises, including, in 2006, imaginative and color-rich Erté-inspired costumes that represent the four seasons.

Bethany and Electra were popular, but it was Helen's third new doll—little seven-and-a-half-inch Riley—that became a star. She was introduced in August 2003 at the annual UFDC convention.

"We needed something for our sales table at UFDC, and we needed it fast!" the artist explains. "I had this little wax model in my studio, saved from molds that we had made for a porcelain edition (the Kish Confections, later known as the Sweethearts). I used the same body, legs

The Girls of Many Lands collection was sculpted by the artist for Pleasant Company.

A Kish & Company family photo from 2002: Kassem Hab Hab, who handles many tasks for the company, with Annalise, Tamas and Helen Kish

and arms, and made some changes on the head, sent them off to the factory and had the first hundred pieces back in the nick of time for UFDC. We had no plans to put her into the main line, but it soon became obvious that we had to."

After the UFDC event, Riley's pictures were posted on various Internet sites, including eBay, and collectors—particularly those who favor fashion dolls—immediately began clamoring to own a Riley of their own. Within a year, her face had appeared in every major magazine for doll collectors. Seemingly overnight, she had become "the little darling of fashion doll collectors," Robert Tonner says.

What is especially amazing about the success of Riley is that she is not like most fashion dolls. She is neither sophisticated nor svelte. Yet, this chubby-cheeked imp stole hearts—and dollars—away from long-limbed vinyl and plastic glamour goddesses like Mattel's Barbie, Robert Tonner's Tyler, Alexander Doll Company's

Cissy and Ashton-Drake's Gene. How did it happen?

The first reason for Riley's success, suggested Robert Tonner in a 2005 interview for *Haute Doll* magazine, is "that she is just so darn cute." He continues, "Riley is a great small size, yet still has Helen's fine sculpted details. Helen has given Riley a real personality, a story and a look that just was not out there."

For the twenty-first-century collector, a fashion doll is much more than a model for stylish clothing. Fashion doll collectors enjoy interacting with their dolls, and Riley's pint-size charm lends her to all manners of adult "play," including creating costumes, setting up displays and photography.

According to her official storyline, Riley is "the twenty-first-century urban toddler." She is three and one-half years of age and lives in an unspecified US city. She attends school at the fictious L'Ecole Gaia, which Helen describes as "the most pretentiously new-age preschool her parents can afford."

Sketch of 1800 West 33rd Street in downtown Denver: home of Kish & Company

Helen poses with parents Donald and Doris Nalty, daughter Annalise and company jack-of-all-trades Kassem Hab Hab in front of Kish & Company in 2004.

In 2004, Helen added Riley to her Whimsies line. Eight Riley dolls were introduced that year, along with a pig-tailed pal named Tulah. In 2005, more than a dozen Rileys were released, both in the LadyKish Whimsies retail line and in conjunction with events and special projects (such as elfin North Pole Riley, which accompanied Joan Muyskens Pursley's book, *Christmas Dolls,* for Reverie Publishing). Riley's world expanded as well, with the addition of neighborhood chums Avery and baby sister Ellery (named after the granddaughters of Denver Doll Emporium's Paula Reding); Zsu Zse, an Asian-born girl; Anjali, Riley's pen pal from India; and DJ, Riley's cousin and the first boy to join her rapidly expanding circle.

The 2006 line, just released as this volume went to press, is similarly rich with Riley and friends. Riley's guises include a 1930s-inspired nurse; DJ appears as a firefighter; and Anjali dons a NASA uniform. And this is only the beginning: other Riley dolls will appear through-out the year at various events. The Kishes have also launched a group of resin Riley figurines, which they hope will appeal to the giftware market.

"I believe that Riley will prove to be the doll that changed the face of doll collecting," says Paula Reding. "We went from collecting never-removed-from-box dolls that were only enjoyed because you knew you had one in a box somewhere, to hands-on, change the clothes, re-wig, buy accessories for, carry with you on vacation: a real play doll for us older children at heart!"

Riley has even helped her maker to re-discover her own inner child. Designing Riley's fun wardrobe, which includes party dresses, tutus and exercise clothing, some-times makes Helen feel "like a designer who has entered her second childhood." (Beginning in 2003, Helen began designing all clothing for the Whimsies line; Rosemarie Ionker continues to design costumes, based on the artist's sketches, for the Signature Edition dolls.)

"I love designing for Riley," the artist says. "It's almost as though she tells me what she likes, but the best part

A face to love: introduced in 2000, vinyl Bethany, 12 inches, would later morph into the smaller Bitty Bethany.

Morning becomes Electra, as does summertime: here the 16-inch vinyl doll poses as the Spirit of Summer.

is that she looks good in almost anything. It's her attitude, I think."

Helen Kish: The Woman and the Artist

Dolls often inspire joy, but the doll business, like any competitive field, is far from fun and games. Since the passing of the heyday of doll collecting (the mid-1980s through mid-1990s), many favorite artists, top companies and successful shops have struggled, faded and disappeared. Yet, Helen Kish, the woman who did not even know that a girl could be an artist, has survived.

What accounts for the artist's longevity? Author and editor Krystyna Poray Goddu, who has observed Helen Kish's artistic evolution since the mid-1980s, points to a combination of three elements—artistry, design and personal compassion. She says, "Helen, like a handful of dollmakers who are both artistically and commercially successful and enduring, is at heart a fine artist. The consistently high quality of her work begins with her talent as a sculptor. Whatever the subject matter, her work has always been characterized by an aesthetic of elegance and harmony. This is reflected in her designs, which are executed with the highest degree of excellence in every aspect: concept, design, proportion, color, texture and line."

Goddu continues: "The immediate, emotional appeal of her dolls has its roots in her compassionate heart and warm nature. Helen is a kind and gracious human being as well as a talented fine artist and skilled designer. When these three aspects of her being come together in a creation, the results are exceptional."

Paula Reding also credits the woman behind the dolls. She says, "Helen is not only a tremendously talented artist, she is also a genuinely nice person. I fondly remember Helen at my granddaughter Ellery's second birthday party. After all the kids had eaten their cake and ice cream at and under the kitchen table, my daughters and I were cleaning up little hands and faces. I looked over at Helen, and there she was, on her hands and knees, wiping cake crumbs and ice cream drips off the floor. You've got to love this woman!"

There is a timeless, almost nostalgic quality to Helen Kish's dolls that has no doubt contributed to her long

Elementary Riley (2004) gleefully celebrates her popularity: designed on a whim, the 7 ½-inch charmer has become Helen Kish's most successful vinyl doll.

Sketch of Riley, 2004

standing in a field that can be fickle. (A doll that is highly sought by collectors may end up languishing on a shop shelf a year later.) Never one to embrace transient trends or follow in another designer's comfortable footsteps, Helen has blazed her own unique trail to success, infusing her work with qualities that endure, rather than those that tease the eye, but quickly lose their luster.

"Time after time, Helen hits her mark with memorable, marvelously sculpted moments that can be enjoyed again and again, like happy reminders of past pleasures," muses collector Tim Purk.

In the 1980s, there was a clear difference between Helen Kish's "art" dolls and her "commercial" dolls, both in her mind and in the perception of collectors. Twenty-five years later, the distinction between the two has faded into unity: even a doll like Riley, that is so rich in "play" qualities, still expresses Helen's artistic nature as fully as one of her works in bronze.

"I no longer see any distinction between the part of me that sculpts a model to become a doll, then goes on to design the necessary accoutrements, and the part of me that sculpts a one-of-a-kind piece," the artist acknowledges. "At my stage of life, there is neither time nor inclination to make intellectual distinctions between 'art' dolls and 'play' dolls: I just do what I do."

As an artist whose inner creative force lead her to the dollmaker's life, Helen Kish has left an unmistakable mark on the culture of doll collecting. Like a classic novel that one reads over and over again, each time discovering new delights, her porcelain and vinyl dolls offer their owners years of fascination and joy. Had Helen Kish retired in 2006, she would have left behind a body of work worthy of the lifetimes of several dollmakers combined.

Even the artist herself, when pressed, admits that should she have to stop producing dolls, she would be content with what she has done so far. "But I would still try to bargain with God for *just one more*," Helen Kish says in earnest. "Martha Armstrong-Hand once said it's okay to do just one thing—just do it well. The one constant for me has been making dolls. I still get a thrill from it."

The resin Raggedy Riley figurine collection was introduced in 2006.

The artist airbrushes doll cheeks in 2002.

The Helen Kish Catalog

The following pages present the majority of the dolls created by Helen Kish, dating from the beginning of her career as a dollmaker in the mid-1970s through early 2006. The catalog offers a comprehensive review of the artist's porcelain and vinyl limited-edition and one-of-a-kind creations, as well as rare glimpses of prototypes and hand-drawn sketches. A generous sampling of the artist's other creative efforts is displayed as well, such as bronze figures, stoneware sculptures, mixed-media compilations and handmade jewelry.

The pieces are exhibited in twelve sections: Early Efforts, A Decade of Porcelains, Designing Woman, A Vinyl Venture Begins, The Vinyl Line Grows Up, Sculptures in Stoneware, Bronze Beauties, Later Porcelain Works, Expressions & Experiments, Later Vinyl Works: Signature Editions, Later Vinyl Works: Lady Kish & the Whimsies and The Life of Riley. Within each section, the dolls are usually shown in chronological order, allowing the reader to trace and examine the evolution of the artist's work. (In a few cases, dolls appear out of chronological order because they share a common trait or theme.)

The rich body of work presented here is a testament to more than thirty years of experimentation, diligence and, most important, devotion. For Helen Kish's success is the result of a lifelong love affair with the study and re-creation of the human form.

Early Efforts

(1975-1982)

Helen Kish's earliest creations, like those of many dollmakers, were influenced in part by the look of antique French and German porcelain dolls. Her first all-original porcelain doll, Aimée, dates from 1975. A wide-eyed, broad-cheeked toddler, Aimée appeared in various costumes and hairstyles over several years.

In addition to making a number of cute but typical-looking toddlers, Helen also endeavored early on to sculpt dolls of personality and character. In 1978, she completed a striking porcelain portrait doll that depicted artist Mary Cassatt; that same year, she sculpted a caricature of one of her uncles. The latter received more praise and attention than any of her previous creations, and launched her in a new direction. From that point on, dollmaking would no longer be only a hobby or craft, but a pursuit of an artistic identity. By 1981, Helen's achievements would be recognized with acceptance into the National Institute of American Doll Artists (NIADA), a prestigious, peer-juried organization for makers of original dolls.

Aimée, porcelain head, arms and legs with cloth body, 15 inches, 1975 (the artist's first original porcelain doll)

Hester Street (inspired by vintage photograph above), porcelain heads, arms and legs with cloth bodies, 18 inches and 14 inches, limited to 10, 1978

Molly, porcelain head with composition body, 18 inches, limited to 2, 1977

Tomi, porcelain head, arms and legs with cloth body, 13 ½ inches, limited to 3, 1977 (portrait of the artist's son)

Irenie and Stevie Googly, porcelain heads, arms and legs with cloth bodies, 14 inches, 1977

Aunt Mai Mai, porcelain head, arms and legs with cloth body, 8 inches, limited to 5, 1978

Mary Cassatt, porcelain head, arms and legs with cloth body, 30 inches, limited to 5, 1978

Buffalo Bill, porcelain head, arms and legs with cloth body, 12 inches seated, limited to 3, 1978 (the artist's first commissioned doll)

Marcel Marceau, porcelain head, arms and legs with cloth body, 22 inches, one-of-a-kind, 1979

Self-portrait, porcelain head, arms and legs with cloth body, 13 inches, limited to 2, 1980 (self-portrait of the artist as a young girl)

Uncle Don, porcelain head, arms and legs with cloth body, 16 inches, limited to 15, 1978

Gnome, Sculpey head, arms and legs with cloth body, 9 inches, one-of-a-kind, 1979

Leprechaun,
terra-cotta,
8 inches, one-of-
a-kind, 1980

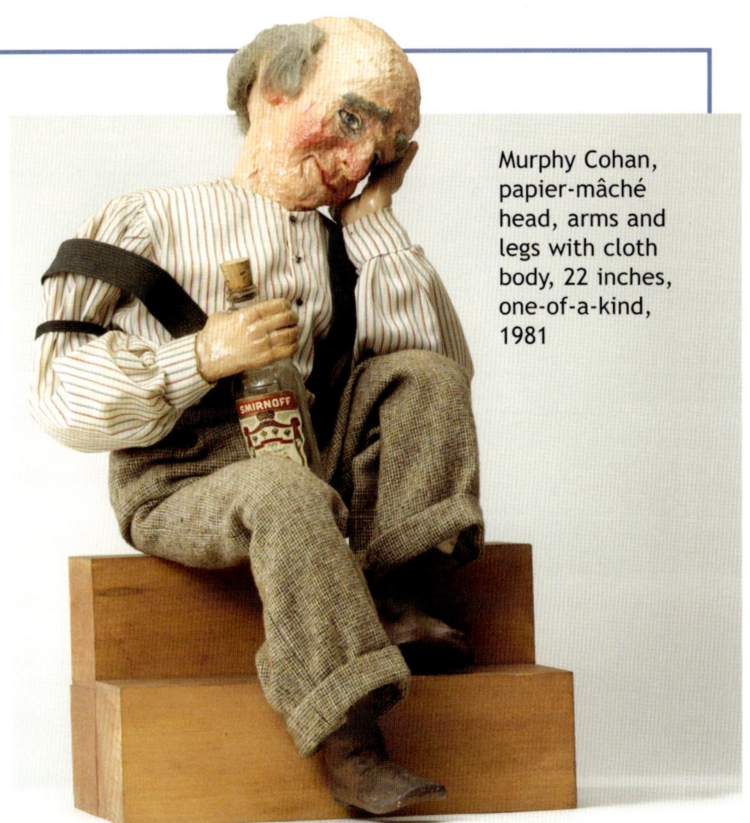

Murphy Cohan,
papier-mâché
head, arms and
legs with cloth
body, 22 inches,
one-of-a-kind,
1981

Pierrot, porcelain
head, arms and
legs with cloth
body, 18 inches,
limited to 10,
1980

Newsboy, porcelain,
13 inches, limited
to 15, 1979 (shown
on the cover of the
March 1980 issue of
The Antiques Journal)

Lise, porcelain,
6 inches, limited
to 15, 1981

Jointed porcelain dolls, 5 to 6 inches, 1981

The Little Match Girl, porcelain head, arms and legs with cloth body, 11 inches, one-of-a-kind, 1981 (the artist's first interpretation of this literary character)

Pouty, porcelain head, arms and legs with cloth body, 16 inches, limited to 10, 1981

The Firebird, porcelain head, arms and legs with cloth body, 21 inches, one-of-a-kind, 1981

Moira Cohan, Sculpey head, arms and legs with cloth body, 20 inches, one-of-a-kind, 1982

Cordelia, porcelain head, arms and legs with cloth body, 21 inches, limited to 15, 1982

Petrouchka, porcelain head, arms and legs with cloth body, 24 inches, limited to 5, 1982

Girl with Molded Cap, porcelain, 9 inches, limited to 2, early 1980s

Hansel and Gretel, porcelain heads, arms and legs with cloth bodies, 14 inches, one-of-a-kind, early 1980s

A Decade of Porcelains

(1983-1993)

Porcelain Children

From 1983 to 1993, the artist continued to hone her skills in porcelain dollmaking. With time, patience and effort, Helen Kish's personal artistic vision took on its own unique shape. Her dolls of children and babies became more lifelike, their expressions soulful. The finely sculpted features became stylized: you can see the pert and appealing bee-stung lips that have since become one of Helen's trademark touches.

That same decade, Helen made some of her most evocative and memorable adult porcelain figures, including the ethereal Victoriana (1983), inspired by Meryl Streep's role in *The French Lieutenant's Woman*; African Madonna (1988), a trio that warmly symbolized a mother's protective love for her children; and Las Mujeres Indigenas (1990), a touching duet that depicted the close relationship between a young Mayan woman and her grandmother. Sculptures like these helped set the high standard for contemporary art dolls, which flourished in the mid-1980s through the mid-1990s.

Laughing Baby and Ryan (from left), jointed porcelain, each 13 inches, limited to 10 (Ryan), 1983 (no more than two Laughing Babies were made)

Tara, porcelain, 13 inches, 1984

Leah, porcelain, 20 inches, limited to 15, 1985

Suzie With Violin, porcelain head, arms and legs with cloth body, 13 inches, limited to 15, 1985

Little Mother and Baby Brother, porcelain, 14 inches and 6 inches, set limited to 150, 1985 (special edition for The Toy Shoppe)

Delia, porcelain, 10 ½ inches, limited to 25, 1988

Molly, porcelain, 10 ½ inches, limited to 25, 1989

Bonita, porcelain, 11 inches, limited to 25, 1992

Bailey, porcelain, 13 inches, one-of-a-kind, 1992

Lennie in Artist's Smock, porcelain, 11 inches, limited to 25, 1991

Lennie in Green Sweater, porcelain, 11 inches, limited to 25, 1991

Porcelain Adults

Diva, porcelain to the waist with leather lower torso, porcelain arms and legs, 30 inches, limited to 3, 1984 (inspired by actress Wihelmenia Wiggins-Fernandez in *Diva*, a 1981 French film)

Victoriana, porcelain head, arms and legs with cloth body, 22 inches, limited to 15, 1983 (shown on the cover of the March/April 1988 issue of *Dolls*; inspired by Meryl Streep's performance in *The French Lieutenant's Woman*)

Victoriana 2, porcelain head, arms and legs with cloth body, 20 inches, limited to 20, 1985

African Madonna 1,
porcelain, 22 inches,
11 inches, and 4 inches,
one-of-a-kind, 1988

African Madonna,
porcelain,
22 inches, 11 inches
and 4 inches,
limited to 25, 1988

Stevie Ray Vaughan, directly modeled
porcelain clay, 21 inches, one-of-a-kind,
1991 (portrait of American blues guitarist,
done as a tribute after his death)

Las Mujeres Indigenas, porcelain,
19 inches and 17 ½ inches,
limited to 12, 1990

La Llorona, directly modeled porcelain
clay with fiber hair, 25 inches, one-of-a-
kind, 1993 (inspired by Mexican-
American legend; the artist also interpreted this piece in stoneware in 1996)

Designing Woman

(From 1984)

Helen Kish's talent was noticed early on not only by collectors and critics, but also by manufacturers and direct-mail companies. By the mid-1980s, Helen had been commissioned to design for R. Dakin & Company and The Franklin Mint. In later years, she worked on projects for The Hamilton Collection, The Danbury Mint and others.

Designing dolls for other companies can be disappointing: prototypes may not be produced, and dolls that *are* released may not be credited to the artist. Yet design work offers an artist the chance to learn how to make dolls that can be mass-produced: Helen's early experiences as a designer would prove invaluable when she launched her own company for the production of vinyl dolls.

Helen's rich experience as a dollmaker and designer was also key to her selection, in 2001, by the Pleasant Company, creator of The American Girls Collection of historically themed dolls and books, to sculpt the Girls of Many Lands, a collection of vinyl dolls with an international theme.

Little Bo Peep, porcelain head, arms and legs with cloth body, 14 inches, early 1980s; prototype for Franklin Heirloom Dolls

Franklin Heirloom Dolls ad for Little Bo Peep, 1988

Gibson Girl, porcelain head, chest plate, arms and legs with cloth body, 20 inches, early 1980s; prototype for The Franklin Mint

The Friendship Garden, wax, 15 inches, early 1980s; model for The Danbury Mint

Danbury Mint product shot for The Friendship Garden, 1980s

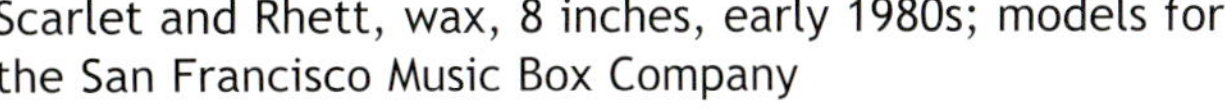

Scarlet and Rhett, wax, 8 inches, early 1980s; models for the San Francisco Music Box Company

Annie Laurie, porcelain, 18 inches, 1984; prototype for R. Dakin & Company

Betsy, porcelain, 10 ½ inches, 1984; prototype for R. Dakin & Company

Meggie, porcelain, 10 inches, 1983; prototype for R. Dakin & Company (Helen's first design for vinyl production)

R. Dakin & Company brochure showing Meggie, 1986

Suzie with Violin, porcelain, 15 inches, 1985; prototype for R. Dakin & Company

The Cowardly Lion, painted wax, 6 inches, 1986; model for The Franklin Mint

The Tin Man, painted wax, 7 ½ inches, 1986; model for The Franklin Mint

The Scarecrow, painted wax, 7 ½ inches, 1986; model for The Franklin Mint

Franklin Mint catalog cover showing the Wizard of Oz dolls, 1986 (Dorothy not designed by Helen Kish)

Elizabeth, porcelain, 18 inches, 1991; prototype for The Hamilton Collection

Ashley ("Grandma's Attic"),
porcelain, 18 inches, 1991;
prototype for The Hamilton
Collection

Cinderella, wax, 5 ½ inches, late
1980s; model for The Franklin Mint

Elizabeth Taylor,
wax, 8 inches,
late 1980s; model for
The Franklin Mint

Shirley Temple, porcelain, 14 inches, 2001; production doll for The Danbury Mint

Shirley Temple, wax, 3 ½ inches, 2000; model for The Danbury Mint

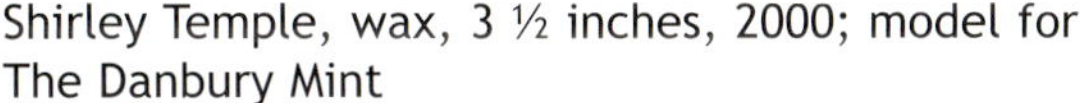

Vanessa, porcelain head, arms and legs with cloth body, 18 inches, 1991; prototype for The Hamilton Collection

Little Doctor, porcelain, 18 inches, 1992; prototype for The Hamilton Collection

French girl, Girls of Many Lands
collection, pencil on paper, 8 inches
by 11 inches, 2001; sketch for
Pleasant Company

English girl, Girls of Many Lands
collection, pencil on paper, 8 inches
by 11 inches, 2001; sketch for
Pleasant Company

Yupik girl, Girls of Many Lands
collection, pencil on paper, 8 inches
by 11 inches, 2001; sketch for
Pleasant Company (this face was not
used in production)

Indian girl, Girls of Many Lands
collection, pencil on paper, 8 inches
by 11 inches, 2001; sketch for
Pleasant Company

Chinese girl, Girls of Many Lands
collection, pencil on paper, 8 inches
by 11 inches, 2001; sketch for
Pleasant Company

Clay studies, oil-based clay, 9 to
12 inches, 2002; samples of different body
sizes for the Girls of Many Lands collection

Spring Pearl, vinyl, 9 ½ inches, 2002
(first vinyl casting for Girls of Many
Lands collection)

Clockwise from lower left: Isabel (England), Leyla (Turkey), Neela (India), Saba (Ethiopia), Kathleen (Ireland), Spring Pearl (China), Cecile (France) and Minuk (Yupik) (center), Girls of Many Lands collection, vinyl, 9 inches, 2002-2003; production dolls for Pleasant Company

A Vinyl Venture Begins

(1991-1995)

Buoyed by the success of her porcelain dolls, Helen Kish was keen to make her work more widely available to collectors. Once armed with the knowledge and skill gleaned from designing dolls for manufacturers, the artist decided to produce her own vinyl dolls. It took years, along with the proverbial sweat and tears, to put her dream into action, but in 1991, Kish & Company was born.

The fledgling company's first offerings were Margie, Mary Kate and Kelsey. Each doll had the same head sculpt, but they were costumed, wigged and painted to represent the style and fashion of a different generation. (Margie represented the 1930s; Mary Kate was reminiscent of the 1950s; and Kelsey was a child of the 1970s.)

With their beautifully detailed, artistic touches (such as handpainted faces and slender, separated fingers) the dolls were a breakthrough in the industry. A few years later, in 1994, Helen's vinyl line boasted a jointing system that allowed movement at the neck, shoulders, elbows, hips and knees. Now her dolls were not only beautiful, unbreakable and affordable, but fully poseable, too.

Kelsey, Mary Kate and Margie (from left), Children of Yesteryear . . . When We Were Little Girls collection, vinyl, 10 ½ inches, each limited to 1,500, 1991 (Kelsey nominated for a 1991 *Dolls* Award of Excellence; all handpainted by the artist)

Sugar, Children of Yesteryear . . . When We Were Little Girls collection, vinyl, 10 ½ inches, limited to 1,500, 1993 (handpainted by the artist; Sugar, along with Andie and Hannah, shown on the cover of the September 1993 issue of *Contemporary Doll Magazine*)

Hannah, Children of Yesteryear . . . When We Were Little Girls collection, vinyl, 10 ½ inches, limited to 1,500, 1993 (handpainted by the artist)

Andie, Children of Yesteryear . . . When We Were Little Girls collection, vinyl, 10 ½ inches, limited to 1,500, 1993 (handpainted by the artist)

Allison and Emmy Lou (from left),
vinyl, 10 ½ inches, each limited to
2,500, 1994

Aimée Lin and Jesse (from left),
All Dressed Up collection, jointed vinyl,
12 ½ inches, each limited to 2,500, 1994

Cara and Whitney (from left), vinyl, 10 ½ inches, each limited to 2,500, 1994

Kristina, All Dressed Up collection, jointed vinyl, 12 ½ inches, limited to 2,500, 1994

Michaela, All Dressed Up collection, jointed vinyl, 12 ½ inches, limited to 2,500, 1994

Nannette, Dance! and Play collection, jointed vinyl,
12 ½ inches, limited to 2,500, 1995

The Little Match Girl, Childhood Favorites collection;
jointed vinyl, 12 ½ inches, limited to 950, 1995 (winner of
a 1995 *Dolls* Award of Excellence)

Willie, Dance! and Play collection, jointed vinyl,
12 ½ inches, limited to 2,500, 1995

Marta, Dance! and Play collection, jointed vinyl,
12 ½ inches, limited to 2,500, 1995

Mary Had a Little Lamb and Little Betty Blue (from left),
Childhood Favorites collection, jointed vinyl, 12 ½ inches,
Little Betty Blue limited to 50 (special edition for
Anything Goes), Mary Had a Little Lamb limited to 150
(special edition for The Toy Shoppe), 1995

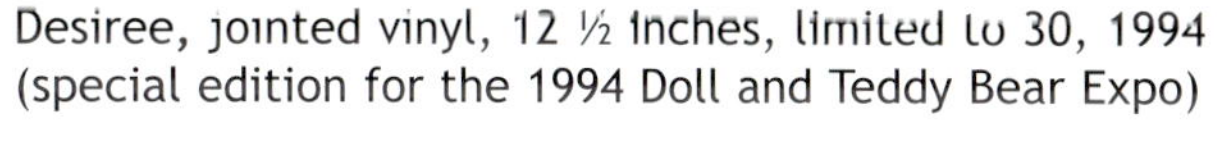

Desiree, jointed vinyl, 12 ½ inches, limited to 30, 1994
(special edition for the 1994 Doll and Teddy Bear Expo)

Penny, Dance! and Play collection, jointed
vinyl, 12 ½ inches, limited to 2,500, 1995
(shown with Jesse, All Dressed Up collection, 1994)

Little Maid, Childhood Favorites
collection, jointed vinyl, 12 ½
inches, limited to 50, 1995 (special edition for Dear Little Dollies)

Little Red Riding Hood, Childhood
Favorites collection, jointed vinyl,
12 ½ inches, limited to 150, 1995
(special edition for The Toy
Shoppe)

The Vinyl Line Grows Up

(1996-1999)

From the mid-1990s to the end of the decade, Helen Kish's vinyl line more than doubled in size. The bulk of the line remained toddlers, but the artist also added babies in 1997 and an adult woman in 1999. Many dolls were introduced in collections built around a theme. Helen tackled some common themes for dolls, such as ballerinas, characters from literature and seasonal clothing. She also came up with some novel ideas, including dolls based on famous paintings by the likes of Mary Cassatt, Pablo Picasso and Pierre Auguste-Renoir.

During this period, the artist's line grew taller as well, with dolls offered in 16-, 20- and 28-inch sizes. The dolls' hairstyles became more varied than in the preceding years, as did the fabrics used for costumes. At the same time, Helen maintained her artistic signature, imbuing her vinyl creations with the same qualities as her handmade originals. You won't find frilly dresses or silly grins in the Kish & Company line, but rather tasteful, well-cut garments and gentle, thoughtful expressions.

Nina, Laura, Lynne, Natalie (clockwise from lower left), Ballerinas collection, vinyl, 10 ½ inches, each limited to 500, 1996 (Lynne nominated for a 1996 *Dolls* Award of Excellence)

Alice and The White Rabbit, vinyl (Alice) and jointed vinyl (White Rabbit), 16 inches and 12 ½ inches, limited to 950 (Alice) and 500 (White Rabbit), 1996 (Alice won a 1996 *Dolls* Award of Excellence)

Tin Woodman, Dorothy, Scarecrow, The Wizard of Oz collection, vinyl (Dorothy), resin (Tin Woodman) and straw (Scarecrow), 12 inches (Scarecrow and Tin Woodman) and 10 ½ inches (Dorothy), limited to 950, 1996 (Wizard of Oz collection nominated for a 1996 *Dolls* Award of Excellence; Scarecrow not made by Kish & Company)

Meredith and MacKenzie (from left), Sunday Best collection, vinyl, 16 inches, each limited to 950; 1996

Molly and Margot (from left), Sunday Best collection, vinyl, 16 inches, each limited to 950, 1996

Victoria Rose, jointed vinyl, 12 ½ inches, limited to 50, 1996 (special edition for Spring House)

Anne of Green Gables, Childhood Favorites collection, jointed vinyl, 12 ½ inches, 1996 (special edition for The Toy Shoppe)

Anne of Green Gables, Childhood Favorites collection, vinyl, 16 inches, limited to 500, 1997

Snow White, Childhood
Favorites collection, vinyl,
16 inches, limited to 500, 1997

Goldilocks, Childhood Favorites collection, vinyl,
12 inches, limited to 750, 1997 (sold in a set with a
10-inch mohair Baby Bear, not shown)

Charlotte, Famous Painters collection, vinyl, 12 inches,
1997 (shown on the cover of the September 1997 issue of
Miniatures, a Spanish publication; inspired by the Mary
Cassatt painting *Playing on the Beach*)

Amalia and Kira (from left), Ballerinas collection, vinyl,
16 inches and 12 inches, each limited to 750, 1997

Mia and Tia (from left), Ballerinas collection, vinyl, 16 inches and 12 inches, each limited to 750, 1997

Rose, Famous Painters collection, vinyl, 16 inches, 1997 (inspired by the James Abbot McNeal Whistler painting *The Little Rose of Lyme Regis*)

Naomi and Tooloo (from left), Sisters collection,
vinyl, 16 inches and 12 inches, limited to 750,
1997

Sara, Famous Painters collection, vinyl,
16 inches, 1997 (inspired by the Mary
Cassatt painting *Child in a Straw Hat)*

White Pierrot and Harlequin ("Picasso Pierrot"), Famous Painters
collection, jointed vinyl, 12 ½ inches, 1997 (Harlequin) and
1998 (White Pierrot) (both inspired by Pablo Picasso paintings of
clowns)

Virginia, vinyl,
16 inches, 1997
(licensed by The
Thomas Jefferson
Memorial
Foundation)

Daphne and Flora (from left),
Sisters collection, vinyl,
16 inches and 12 inches, 1997

Starlight, vinyl, 12 inches, 1997
(inspired by an illustration by Michael
Hague in *The Children's Book
of Virtues*, published by Simon &
Schuster in 1995)

Carolyn, Christening Babies collection, vinyl head, arms and legs with cloth body, 20 inches, limited to 500, 1997

Elizabeth, Christening Babies collection, vinyl head, arms and legs with cloth body, 20 inches, limited to 500, 1997

Margarete ("Loves Me, Loves Me Not") vinyl, 12 inches, limited to 750, 1997

Max, jointed vinyl, 12 ½ inches, one-of-a-kind, 1997 (inspired by *Where the Wild Things Are* by Maurice Sendak; prototype created for FAO Schwarz but not produced)

Beatrice,
Famous
Painters
collection,
jointed vinyl,
12 ½ inches,
1998

Kathy and Kitten (in school attire; from left), vinyl,
16 inches and 12 inches, 1998

Irene, Famous Painters collection, jointed vinyl, 12 ½
inches, limited to 950, 1998 (inspired by the Pierre-
Auguste Renoir painting *Irene Cahan d'Anvers*)

Kathy and Kitten (in country attire; from left), vinyl, 16
inches and 12 inches, 1998

Cassie, Buffy, Patty and
Betsy (from left), vinyl,
10 ½ inches, 1998

Drummer Boy, jointed vinyl, 12 ½ inches,
limited to 30, 1998 (special edition for
Doll and Teddy Bear Expo East)

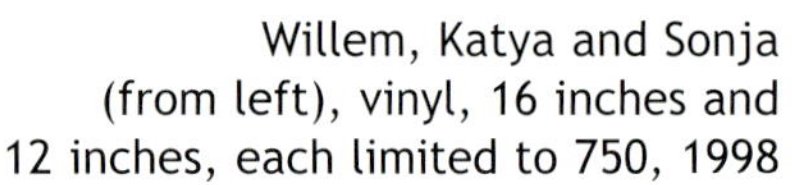

Willem, Katya and Sonja
(from left), vinyl, 16 inches and
12 inches, each limited to 750, 1998

Spring, Winter, Fall and Summer (clockwise from lower left), The Four Seasons collection, 16 inches (Winter, Fall) and 12 inches (Spring, Summer), each limited to 75, 1998 (all handpainted by the artist)

Deirdre and William (from left), vinyl, 12 inches, 1998

Pippi Longstocking, vinyl, 12 inches, limited to 450, 1999 (nominated for a 1999 *Dolls* Award of Excellence)

Blue Pierrot and
Blue Pierrette, Masked
Balls and Carnivals
collection, jointed vinyl,
12 ½ inches, each
limited to 500, 1999

Elizabeth and Polly Dolly, Carolyn and Lolly
Dolly (from left), Babies' Nursery collection,
vinyl heads, arms and legs with cloth
bodies (Elizabeth and Carolyn) and vinyl
with cloth bodies (Polly Dolly and Lolly
Dolly), 20 inches and 10 inches, each
limited to 500, 1999 (shown on the cover of
the June/July 1999 issue of *Dolls*)

Marisa, Babies' Nursery
collection, vinyl head, arms
and legs with cloth body,
20 inches, limited to 500,
1999 (winner of a 1999 *Doll
Reader* DOTY Award)

Emma, Alicia and Robin (from left),
In an English Garden collection, vinyl,
16 inches and 12 inches, limited to
500 (Emma and Alicia) and 250
(Robin), 1999

Isabelle Rose, In an English Garden collection, vinyl, 28 inches, limited to 250, 1999 (winner of a 1999 *Dolls* Award of Excellence; shown with Emma, Alicia and Robin)

Sculptures in Stoneware

(From 1994)

In the early 1990s, eager to expand her artistic repertoire, Helen Kish began experimenting with stoneware. "I love the feel of it; I love the texture," she said in 1994 at the formal debut (at the 32nd annual NIADA conference) of one of her earliest stoneware sculptures, The Sentinel.

Helen relishes the process, albeit challenging, of finding form in stoneware clay. She explains, "I love the process of adding to and taking away, watching it dry to bone hardness and, finally, trusting it to the fire. It's immediate—there are no molds, no wax models to tweak. And it is risky: there's no backup if the piece blows up in the kiln."

To differentiate her stoneware and bronze pieces from her porcelain and vinyl dolls, Helen adopted another artistic signature: Helen Cunalta Kish. (Cunalta is an old Gaelic family name.) Works from the Cunalta Kish Studio are born of the artist's most contemplative and personal thoughts, and are often inspired by poetry.

The Sentinel, stoneware, papier-mâché, cloth and paper, 26 inches, one-of-a-kind, 1994

Sweet Home Chicago, stoneware, fiber and wood, 36 inches, one-of-a-kind, 1994

Maiden, stoneware, fiber and beads,
14 inches, one-of-a-kind, 1996

The Turn ("He Who Vanquished the Mother of His Fears"), stoneware,
fiber and leather, 24 inches, one-of-a-kind, 1995 (inspired by an
interpretation of *Beowulf* by David Whyte; produced in bronze in 1996)

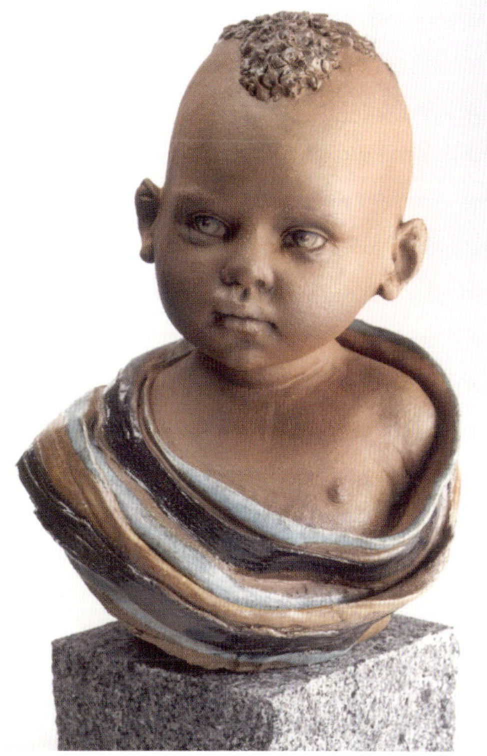

Child of the Nomad, stoneware,
8 ½ inches, one-of-a-kind, 1996

La Llorona Supplicant, stoneware and fiber, 15 inches, one-of-a-kind, 1996 (inspired by Mexican-American legend; the artist's first interpretation of "La Llorona" was made in porcelain in 1993)

La Llorona Supplicant, front view of clay drying

Roses Have Thorns, stoneware and fiber, 24 inches, one-of-a-kind, 1997 (inspired by the poem "The Wind, One Brilliant Day" by Antonio Machado)

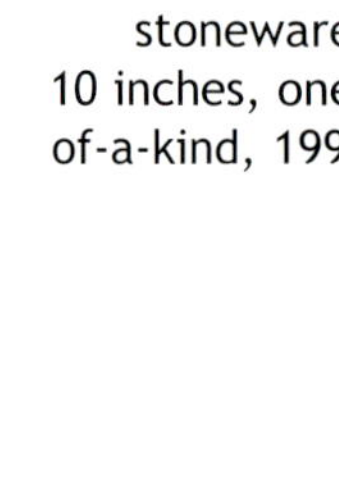

Rosebud, stoneware, 10 inches, one-of-a-kind, 1997

Putto, stoneware and fiber, 11 inches, one-of-a-kind, 1998

Bliss ("Joy as it Flies"), stoneware and silk, 13 inches, one-of-a-kind, 1997 (with The Captive, inspired by the poem "Eternity" by William Blake)

The Captive, stoneware, silk and silver, 14 inches, one-of-a-kind, 1997 (with Bliss, inspired by the poem "Eternity" by William Blake)

Artist's Model, stoneware, 20 inches, one-of-a-kind, 1997 (quote from novelist Dorothy L. Sayers inscribed on base)

Ennui, stoneware and fiber, 18 inches, one-of-a-kind, 1999

Columbine Song, stoneware and fiber, 20 inches, one-of-a-kind, 1999
(created to commemorate the Columbine High School killings of April 20, 1999;
the poem "Forget Your Life" by Rumi written on figures)

Phoenix, stoneware, 28 inches,
one-of-a-kind, 1998 (stanza from
Rainer Maria Rilke's poem
"My Life Is Not This Steeply Sloping
Hour" inscribed on base)

I bring you with reverent hands
The books of my numberless dreams
White woman that passion has worn
As the tide wears the dove-grey sands

— *W.B. Yeats*

White Woman,
pencil on paper,
12 inches by
16 inches, 2000

White Woman, stoneware and silk, 22 inches,
one-of-a-kind, 2000 (inspired by the poem "A Poet
to His Beloved" by W.B. Yeats)

Bronze Beauties

(From 1996)

Helen Kish's bronze creations, like her stoneware works, are born of dreams. They often depict fairies, angels and mythic creatures and characters. The artist began producing bronze pieces in the mid-1990s, but her interest in the medium began in her college days. Says Helen, "From the time I took my first art history class, I wanted to understand how bronze was made. I could only dream then of seeing something of my own making cast in the ancient material."

To have a work produced in bronze, Helen turns over her sculpture, formed in either terra-cotta or industrial clay, first to a specialized moldmaker, then to a foundry for casting and finishing. The process is both time-consuming and costly. "By the time it was financially possible for me to get a piece cast in bronze, I had learned another useful skill— letting go," the artist says.

Helen has produced bronzes in a variety of finishes, including antique-look brown and green patinas. Some pieces are painted with acrylics, or "polychromed," for a more contemporary look.

The Turn ("He Who Vanquished the Mother of His Fears"), bronze, 15 ½ inches, limited to 35, 1996 (inspired by an interpretation of *Beowulf* by David Whyte)

Long Flight Home, bronze, 7 inches high by 10 inches wide, limited to 35, 1996

Manitou, bronze, 14 inches, limited to 10, 1996

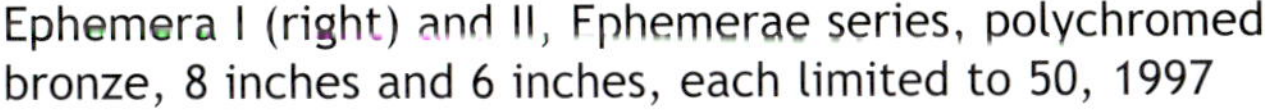

Dreaming Girl, bronze, 17 inches long by 7 inches high, limited to 10, 1997

Ephemera I (right) and II, Ephemerae series, polychromed bronze, 8 inches and 6 inches, each limited to 50, 1997

Ephemera II with French bronze patina

Meditation on a Swing, bronze, 6 inches, limited to 12, 1998

Eve, bronze, 22 inches, limited to 10, 1997

Newborn Angel, bronze, 6 ½ inches, limited to 50, 1997

Guardian of Little Angels, 20 inches, bronze, limited to 12, 1998 (tribute to Janet Marchese, former owner of The Angel Keeper and advocate for children with Down's Syndrome; quote from Mother Teresa inscribed on base)

Selkie, bronze, 12 inches, limited to 12, 1998

Ephemera III, Ephemerae series, bronze, 6 inches, limited to 50, 1999; shown with a multi-colored patina of verde brown and Dutch blue (left) and with French brown patina (right)

Ephemera IV, Ephemerae series, bronze, 10 ½ inches, limited to 50, 1999

Ephemera V, Ephemerae series, bronze, 7 inches long by 4 inches high, limited to 50, 2001 (shown with a multi-colored patina of antique burgundy and Chinese brown)

Ephemera VI, Ephemerae series, bronze, 5 inches, limited to 50, 2001

Later Porcelain Works

(From 1994)

When Helen Kish began to make dolls, porcelain was her primary medium. As her career evolved, however, the demanding process of porcelain dollmaking often took a back seat to other projects. From 1991 to 1994, Helen served as president of NIADA, and as she handled myriad responsibilities for the organization, her artistic output was reduced. Also in the early 1990s, Helen was developing and launching her vinyl doll line. Later in that decade, she stretched her creative wings and experimented with stoneware, bronze and other means of artistic expression.

Still, the artist always found a pocket of time to make porcelain dolls, even if as few as one or two a year. The creations in this section run the gamut from unusual one-of-a-kind pieces, such as Baby Godiva (and Peeping Tom) from 1999—which manages to be evocative and adorable at the same time—to small editions, such as impish baby angel Winged Veronica (1999).

"Porcelain, like bronze, has an ancient pedigree," Helen says. "It is a beautiful medium … timeless. I'll always love porcelain."

Miguelito, porcelain, 11 ½ inches, one-of-a-kind, 1994 (donated as a "helper" at the 32nd annual NIADA conference)

Shannon, porcelain, 11½ inches, one-of-a-kind, 1995

Michael Lauren,
porcelain,
8 inches, limited
to 35, 1998
(came in trunk
with seven
outfits)

Tomi with Fairy, porcelain heads, arms and legs with cloth
bodies, 18 inches and 5 inches, one-of-a-kind, 1996

Juliette, left, and Emilie, porcelain, 13 inches and 10
inches, each limited to 35, 1997 (shown on the cover of
the October 1997 issue of *Doll Reader*)

Winged Veronica, porcelain, 10 inches,
limited to 10, 1999 (special edition for The
Angel Keeper)

Winged Veronica, pencil on paper,
12 inches by 16 inches, 1999

Bride of the Sea, porcelain head, arms and legs with cloth
body, 27 inches, limited to 10, 1997

Cissie, porcelain, 11 inches, limited to 60, 1996

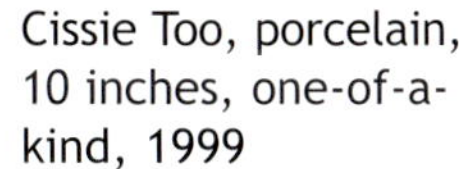

Cissie Too, porcelain, 10 inches, one-of-a-kind, 1999

Cissie Blue, porcelain, 10 inches, one-of-a-kind, 1999

Baby Godiva and Peeping Tom, porcelain (Baby Godiva) and porcelain with Paperclay costume (Peeping Tom), 13 inches and 3 ½ inches, one-of-a-kind, 1999

Baby Veronica, porcelain, 10 inches, one-of-a-kind, 1999

Jacob and Lindy, porcelain, 10 inches,
each limited to 35, 1998

Sophie, porcelain, 7 ½ inches, 1998 (collaboration with Robert Tonner; produced by Tonner Doll Company for the 36th annual NIADA conference)

Bonnie, porcelain, 13 inches, limited to 35, 1998

Delaney, porcelain, 11 ½ inches, limited to 35, 1998

Amanda and Abigail, porcelain (Amanda), porcelain head with cloth body (Abigail), 11 inches and 4 inches, set limited to 20, 2000

Marley and Dolly, porcelain heads, arms and legs with cloth bodies, 18 inches and 7 inches, set limited to 25, 2000

Delaney Too, porcelain, 11 ½ inches, limited to 20, 2004 (sold with Bebe Kishlet, vinyl head, arms and legs with cloth body, 4 ½ inches)

Silver Spoon, porcelain head with cloth body, 4 inches, limited to 12, 2001 (special edition for Distinctive Doll)

Fidelio, porcelain, 11 inches, one-of-a-kind, 2002

Little Raven, porcelain, 6 ½ inches, limited to 12, 2004

Estike (top); Candy Cane
and Liebkuchken (middle row,
from left); and Lollipop,
Sweet Pea and Bon Bon
(bottom row, from left),
Sweethearts collection,
porcelain, 6 inches, each
limited to 25, 2004 (special
edition for Denver Doll
Emporium; these characters
were initially—and briefly—
offered in 2000 as the Kish
Confections; they are
also the forerunners
of Riley)

Expressions &
Experiments

(From 1992)

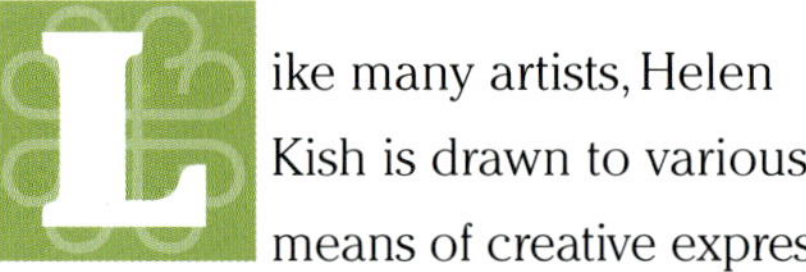

ike many artists, Helen Kish is drawn to various means of creative expression. As this chapter shows, she has created wee figurines, sculptures in various media, decorative ornaments and jewelry. "I do need a break from dolls now and then," the artist admits with a smile. "Making jewelry and other one-of-a-kind pieces affords me the satisfaction of creating something from beginning to end; there is an immediacy that isn't possible with a production piece."

Oftentimes her creative experiments are offshoots of her doll projects. Helen's pins for the Kish Collectors' Society (2001, 2002; the artist's fan club) were inspired by her dolls' faces, and her Raggedy Riley figurines (2006) are an outgrowth of her phenomenally successful vinyl Riley doll. Other times, the pieces evolve spontaneously. "The little Star Babies [1999] made their appearance when I was bedridden for a week with some odious virus. I kept some clay on my nightstand and these little models just started popping out—they helped me get well!" Helen says.

Sculptures, ornaments and figurines

Bust of Woman, porcelain, 6 ½ inches, 1992 (souvenir for the 30th annual NIADA conference; shown on the cover of *The Art of the Doll*, published by NIADA in 1992)

Black Harlequin, jointed
porcelain, 9 inches,
limited to 2, 1997

Angel Bas-relief, terra-cotta, tile and wood, 17 inches wide by 23 inches high, one-of-a-kind, 1997

Garden Girl, resin bas-relief, 9 inches wide by 11 inches high, limited to 2, 1995

Richard, oil-based clay, 8 inches, one-of-a-kind, 2000

Baby in Hands, resin bas-relief, 6 ½ inches wide by 9 inches high, 2000 (inspired by a photograph of the artist's hands holding a doll head, shown on the cover of the 1999 Kish & Company catalog)

Bas-relief on Wood, epoxy (sculpture) and wood (base), 6 inches high by 18 inches wide, one-of-a-kind, 2000

Classic, Suddenly Shy and Take Five (from left), Raggedy Riley collection, painted resin, 3 ½ inches long (Classic, Take Five) and 5 inches high (Suddenly Shy), 2006

Kish Collectors' Society pin, bas-relief porcelain baby, 2 ½ inches, 2000 (face is same as that of baby held by Marley, one of the artist's porcelains from 2000)

Star Babies, painted resin (front) and clay (back), 2 ½ to 5 inches, 1999

Emersen's Special Box, resin figure on purchased wooden box, 3 inches (figure), one-of-a-kind, 2005

Winged Angel,
resin, 5 inches,
2000

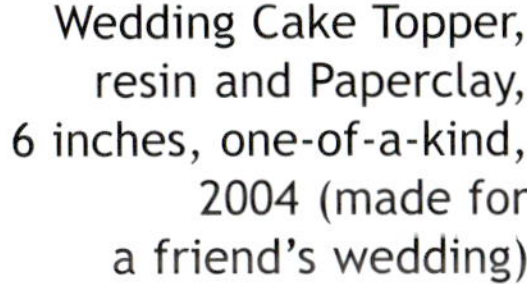

Wedding Cake Topper,
resin and Paperclay,
6 inches, one-of-a-kind,
2004 (made for
a friend's wedding)

Angel plate, wax model, 8 inches (diameter), one-of-a-kind, 2000

Lyric Angel, resin bas-relief, 12 inches wide by 11 inches high, 2005 (prototype for a project in development)

Lyric Angel, pencil on paper,
9 inches by 12 inches, 2003

Jewelry

Fairy collar, resin fairies center with triple strand of semi-precious green stones, 16 inches, one-of-a-kind, 2000

Art Deco necklace, vintage brass stamping on jet, gold wire collar, 16 inches, one-of-a-kind, 2004

Baby in hand pin, gold-wire-wrapped resin, beads and fresh-water pearls, 2 inches, one-of-a-kind, 2001 (made for the Kish Collectors' Society, 2002-2003)

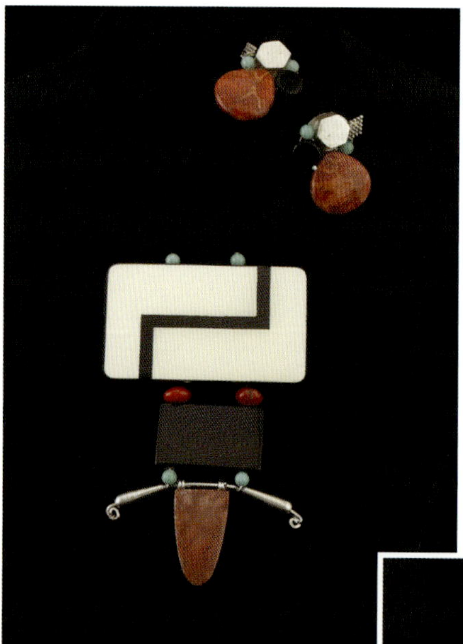

Buckle brooch, vintage plastic buckle, jet, aventurine and jasper, 3 inches, one-of-a-kind, 2004 (shown with matching earrings of coral, aventurine and silver)

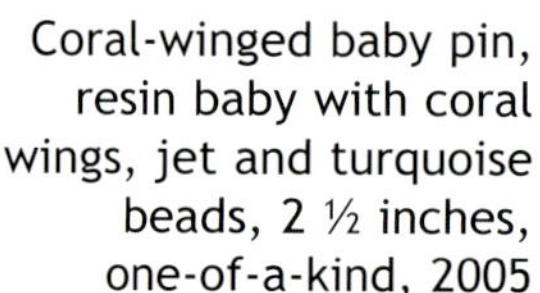

Celtic pin, ceramic pin from Ireland wrapped in gold wire, beads and fresh-water pearls, 2 inches, one-of-a-kind, 2000

Coral-winged baby pin, resin baby with coral wings, jet and turquoise beads, 2 ½ inches, one-of-a-kind, 2005

Lapis and turquoise pendant, lapis glass stone wrapped in gold wire with turquoise and gold beads, 1 ¼ inches (diameter), 2002

Silver and lapis earrings, rectangular lapis beads with silver coins, 1 ¼ inches, one-of-a-kind, 2005

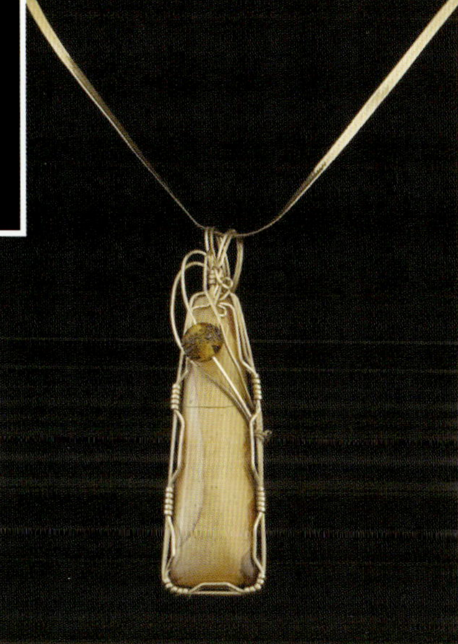
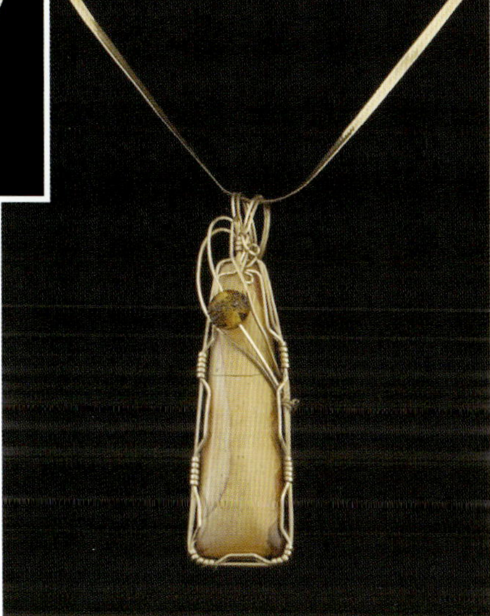

Wrapped stone pendant, teardrop Utah picture stone wrapped in gold wire, gold chain, one-of-a-kind, 2-inch pendant, 2000

Blue topaz necklace, topaz and silver, 14 inches, one-of-a-kind, 2004 (shown with matching earrings)

Chalecedony and annular necklace, chalcedony center stone wrapped in gold wire with double strand of citrine and Venetian glass annulars, 16 inches, one-of-a-kind, 2002

Beaded crochet collar, beads, freshwater pearls and 32-gauge silver wire, 16 inches, one-of-a-kind, 2005 (shown with matching earrings)

Later Vinyl Works: Signature Editions

(From 2000)

In 2000, Helen Kish divided her vinyl line into two categories: the Signature Editions collection and the LadyKish collection. The Signature Editions group was conceived as a sophisticated, higher-end line that would include limited-edition pieces hand finished by the artist herself. The LadyKish dolls, in contrast, would be designed and aimed at a broader collector market.

For themes for her Signature Editions, the artist has turned to some favorite interests: ballet (for Coppelia in 2000 and Spectre de La Rose in 2002), art (Infanta in 2000) and literature (Little Red Riding Hood in 2001 and Sheherazade in 2004). Family history and photographs led to the creation of several pieces, including Veronica (2001) and Teddy (2002), who grace the cover of this book. The Signature Editions collection also includes limited-edition dolls made for the Kish Collectors' Society and several one-of-a-kinds—Who Needs a Wizard? (2003), Birth of Venus, Re-interpreted (2003) and Mixed Metals (2004), which feature Kish & Company dolls that have been cleverly resculpted or reconfigured by Helen.

Coppelia, jointed vinyl, 20 inches, limited to 200, 2000 (inspired by the ballet *Coppélia*; nominated for a 2000 *Dolls* Award of Excellence)

Infanta, vinyl, 10 inches, limited to 200, 2000 (inspired by the painting *Las Meninas* by Velazquez)

Isabelle Rose Wedding Day,
vinyl, 28 inches, one-of-a-kind,
2000 (made for debut in the
book *Here Come the Bride Dolls*
by Louise Fecher, published by
Portfolio Press)

Star Maiden clay
sketch, oil-based
clay, 8 inches high
by 6 inches wide,
1999

Star Maiden, jointed vinyl, 20 inches,
2000 (special edition for the Kish
Collectors' Society; fewer than 200 made)

Kaley, Shannon and Casey (from left),
Treehouse Gang collection, vinyl,
10 inches, each limited to 75, 2001

Milly in floral romper,
2001 (outfit only)

Milly in smocked
turquoise dress,
2001 (outfit only)

Milly, Marty, Molly, Madison and Matty (clockwise from lower left), Kish Quints collection, vinyl, 8 inches, each limited to 100, 2001

Matty in sailor suit, 2001 (outfit only)

Matty in sweater set, 2001 (outfit only)

Marty in plaid overalls, 2001 (outfit only)

Marty in turquoise rompers, 2001 (outfit only)

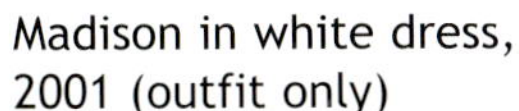

Madison in white dress, 2001 (outfit only)

Madison in butterfly play suit, 2001 (outfit only)

Molly in turquoise sundress, 2001 (outfit only)

Molly in blue dress, 2001 (outfit only)

Carmen, jointed vinyl,
20 inches, limited to 100, 2001
(inspired by the opera Carmen)

Veronica Wilde and baby Lauren
(The Wilde Legacy), jointed vinyl
(Veronica) and vinyl (Lauren), 20 inches
and 8 inches, set limited to 200,
2001 (based on a Kish family portrait)

Little Red Riding Hood, vinyl, 10 inches, limited to 30,
2001 (special edition for Happily Ever After)

Flower Girl and Ringbearer, vinyl, 12 inches,
each limited to 50, 2001

Veronica's Bridal Day, jointed vinyl, 20 inches, limited to 100, 2001 (Veronica interpreted as a 1928 bride; nominated for a 2001 *Doll Reader* DOTY award)

Teddy, Veronica and Lauren (from left), Tea at the Waldorf collection, jointed vinyl (Veronica and Lauren) and vinyl (Teddy), 20 inches, 12 ½ inches and 8 inches, set limited to 100, 2002 (Veronica and Teddy shown on the cover of the September 2002 issue of *Doll,* a British publication)

Kiki and Cosette ("French Girls"), jointed vinyl, 12 ½ inches, each limited to 75, 2002 (Kiki nominated for a 2002 *Dolls* Award of Excellence; both dolls shown on the cover of the March 2002 of *Contemporary Doll Collector*)

Isabelle Rose Bride, vinyl, 28 inches, limited to 25, 2002 (nominated for a 2002 *Dolls* Award of Excellence; close-up of hand shows the doll's beautifully sculpted fingers)

Guv'ner, Treehouse Gang
collection, vinyl, 10 inches,
limited to 75, 2002

Spectre de La Rose, jointed vinyl, 20 inches, limited
to 100, 2002 (inspired by the ballet *Le Spectre de la rose*;
nominated for a 2002 *Doll Reader* DOTY Award)

Lucy and doll, Treehouse Gang collection,
vinyl (Lucy) and cloth (doll), 10 inches and 4 ¼
inches, set limited to 75, 2002 (winner of
a 2002 *Doll Reader* DOTY Award)

Queen of the May
costume sketch, pencil
on paper, 8 inches by
10 inches, 2002

Belle, Bethany and Belinda (from left), Queen of the May
collection, vinyl, 12 inches, each limited to 75, 2003

Boy with doll, vinyl
(boy) and resin with
cloth body (doll),
10 ½ inches and
4 inches, one-of-a-
kind, 2003 (one-of-a-
kind interpretation of
the Hannah doll,
made as a gift)

Blue Moon Baby, vinyl head, arms and
legs with cloth body, 10 inches, 2002 (special
edition for the Kish Collectors' Society;
fewer than 200 made)

Moon Maiden, jointed vinyl,
20 inches, 2002 (special edition for
the Kish Collectors' Society;
fewer than 100 made)

Rebeccah,
Americana
collection,
12 inches, limited
to 75, 2003

Desiree,
Americana
collection, vinyl,
16 inches,
limited to 75,
2003

Jackson, Americana collection, vinyl,
16 inches, limited to 75, 2003

Mariah, Americana collection, vinyl,
16 inches, limited to 75, 2003

Little Deer, Americana collection,
12 inches, limited to 100, 2003

Arabella, left, and Cecily, Renaissance Girls collection, vinyl, 12 inches, each limited to 75, 2004 (shown on the cover of the November/December 2004 issue of *Doll Castle News*)

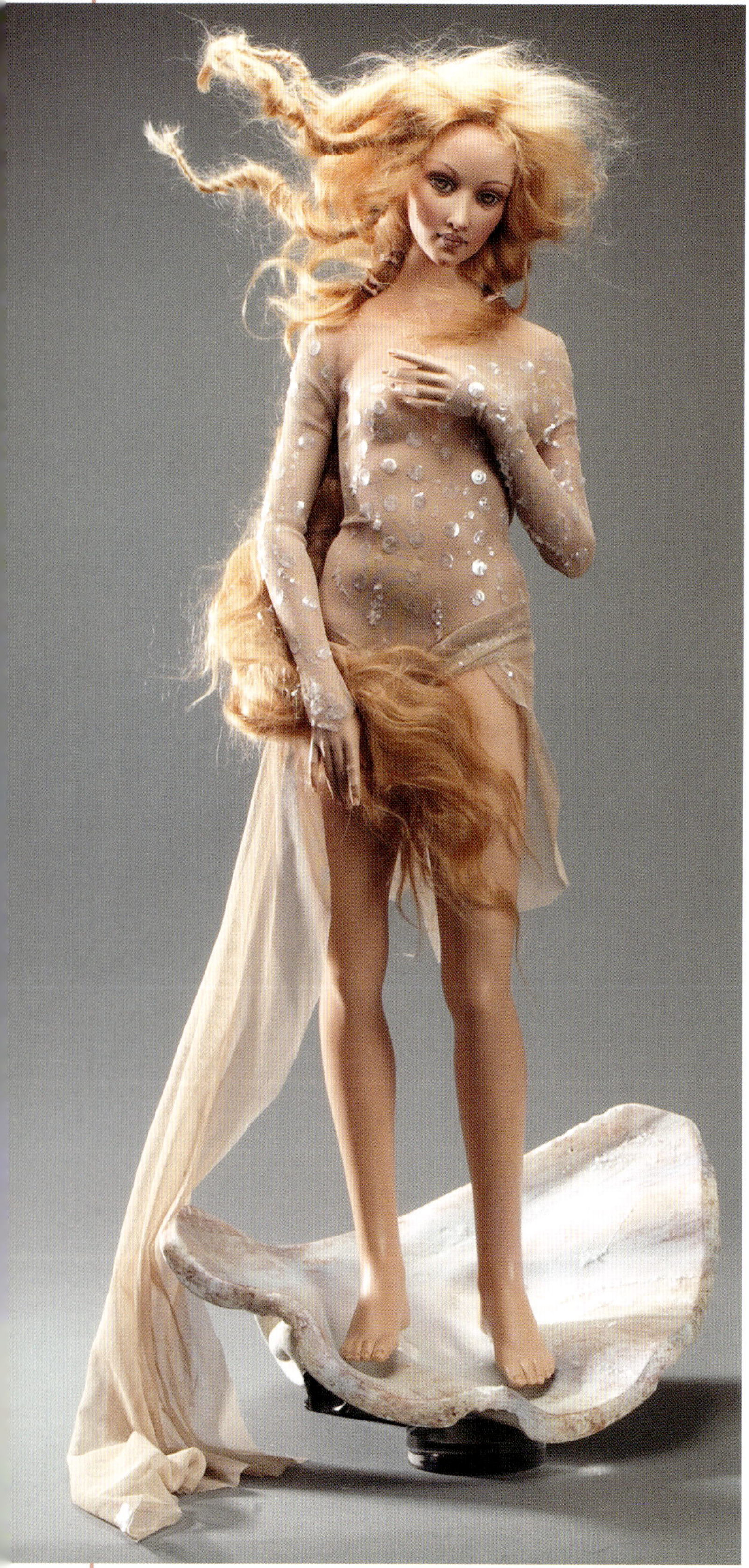

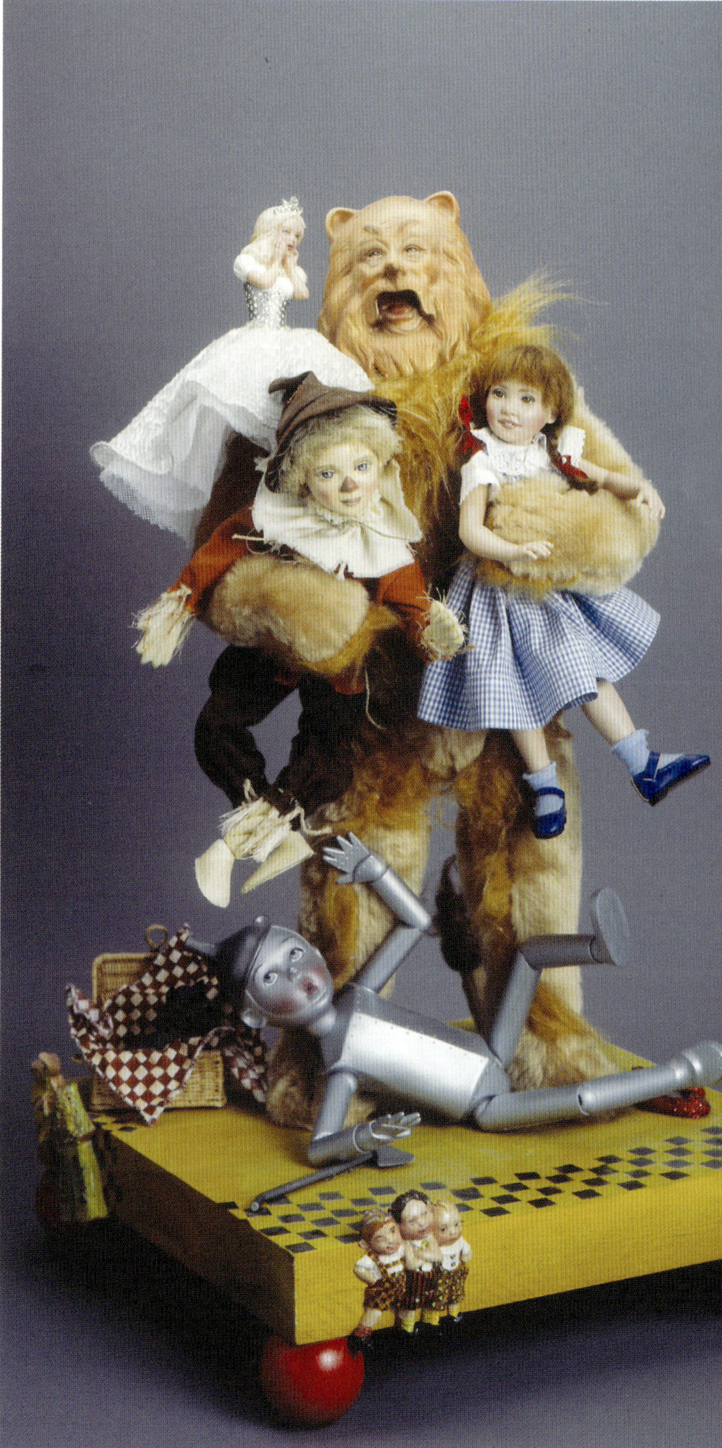

Birth of Venus, Re-interpreted, vinyl, 28 inches, one-of-a-kind, 2003 (the Isabelle Rose doll remodeled to represent Botticelli's *Birth of Venus*; doll's face was reshaped, arms were cut, repositioned and resurfaced with modeling epoxy; piece made for a gallery display at IDEX)

Who Needs a Wizard (when you have friends)?, mixed media, 24 inches, one-of-a-kind, 2003 (lion, a blend of porcelain, cloth and faux fur, holds Kish & Company Wizard of Oz collection from 1996; one-of-a-kind Glinda, made of resin and cloth, whispers into the lion's ear; base is wood, painted and adorned with resin appliqués sculpted by the artist to represent characters from Oz)

Mixed Metals, mixed media, 16 inches, one-of-a-kind, 2004 (auctioned at IDEX for $3,600, piece includes one-of-a-kind interpretation of the Electra doll with sculpted resin hair and bodice, metal peplum and silver skirt; backdrop is part of a crèche display and is metal and glass)

Mixed Metals costume sketch, pencil on paper, 8 ½ inches by 11 inches, 2003

Sheherazade costume sketch, pencil on paper, 8 ½ inches by 11 ½ inches, 2003

Sheherazade, jointed vinyl, 20 inches, limited to 100, 2004

Later Vinyl Works: LadyKish & the Whimsies

(From 2000)

The LadyKish line, established in 2000, was named after a pet moniker given to Helen Kish by fitness guru Richard Simmons, an enthusiastic doll collector. In 2003, the line was renamed the LadyKish Whimsies to suggest charm, delight and wonder—the qualities found in the dolls produced therein. Like the Signature Editions, the Whimsies are limited, but edition sizes are larger, typically ranging from 300 and up.

The LadyKish line boasts a bevy of cutie-pies and cutie-patooties. They include Bethany, a 12-inch toddler and the first newly sculpted doll to debut in the line. Neat and sweet (in the Confections collection, she depicts a variety of sugary goodies), Bethany later became petite, as she morphed into an 11-inch size—Bitty Bethany—in 2003. The wee "Kishlets," precious baby dolls that measure just 4 ½ inches, were born in 2003 as well. That same year, the line's most popular toddler yet, Riley, made her infamous debut.

The Whimsies are not all fun and games, however. The elegant Electra, a 16-inch lady, was introduced in 2003 as an event souvenir, but was soon added to the regular line.

Bethany, vinyl, 12 inches, limited to 1,500, 2000 (shown with separately available costumes)

Cotton Candy, Blueberry Jam and Taffy (bottom row, from left), Butterscotch, Peach Parfait (middle row, from left) and Lollipop (top), Confections collection, vinyl, 12 inches, Lollipop limited to 30; others limited to 300, 2000 (all the Confections are the Bethany doll; Lollipop was a special edition for the 2000 Doll and Teddy Bear Expo East)

Butterscotch Bethany, Confections collection, vinyl, 12 inches, limited to 300, 2000 (nominated for a 2000 *Dolls* Award of Excellence and won a 2000 *Doll Reader* DOTY Award)

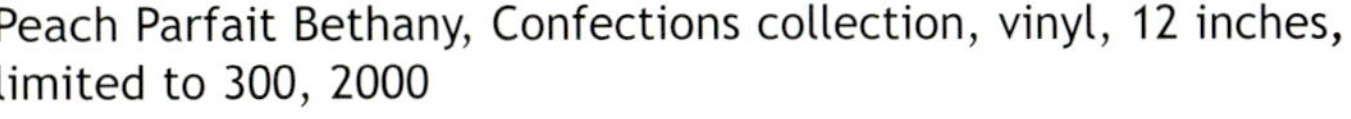

Peach Parfait Bethany, Confections collection, vinyl, 12 inches, limited to 300, 2000

Bethany (brunette), vinyl, 12 inches, limited to 1,500, 2000

Christopher, vinyl,
12 inches, limited to 1,500,
2000

Jo (brunette), vinyl,
16 inches, limited to 1,500,
2000

Jack, vinyl, 16 inches,
limited to 1,500, 2000

Jo (blonde), vinyl, 16 inches,
limited to 1,500, 2000

Rachel, vinyl,
16 inches,
limited to
1,500, 2000

Bethany, Jo, Christopher and Jack (from left), Home for the Holidays collection, vinyl, 16 inches (Jo, Jack) and 12 inches (Bethany, Christopher), each limited to 300, 2000

Alpine Bluebell, Columbine, Scotch Pine, Autumn Aspen, Indian Paintbrush and High Prairie Rose (from top), Rocky Mountain Highlands collection, vinyl, 16 inches, each limited to 300, 2000 (High Prairie Rose is the Rachel doll; all others are the Jo doll)

Marley and Kate, vinyl heads, arms and legs with cloth bodies, 20 inches and 10 inches, set limited to 1,500, 2000 (shown on the cover of the August/September 2000 issue of *Doll*, a British publication)

Divinity, Cherry Pie and Almond Toffee (from left), Confections collection, vinyl, 12 inches, each limited to 300, 2001 (all the Confections are the Bethany doll)

Ni' night Bethany, vinyl, 12 inches, limited to 10, 2001(special edition for The Friend Company)

Savannah, vinyl, 10 inches, limited to 25, 2001 (special edition for the 2001 Doll and Teddy Bear Expo East)

Marley Anne, Marley Jo and Marley
Beth (from left), Marley's Slumber
Party collection, vinyl heads,
arms and legs with cloth bodies,
20 inches, each limited to 100, 2001

Bethany, Christopher and Jo (from left), Christmas Morning collection, vinyl, 16 inches (Jo) and 12 inches (Bethany, Christopher), each limited to 75, 2002

Penelope and her doll, vinyl (Penelope) and vinyl head, arms and legs with cloth body (doll), 10 inches and 4 inches, set limited to 300, 2002

Bethany and her doll, Christmas Morning collection (detail), doll is resin with cloth body, 4 inches, limited to 75, 2002

Bethany Bear, vinyl with resin mask, 12 inches, 2002 (special edition for the Kish Collectors' Society; fewer than 100 made)

Butterfly Kisses
Bethany in event
companion
ensemble, limited
to 50 (outfit only)

Carolyn and Cassie,
vinyl head, arms and
legs with cloth
bodies, 20 inches and
10 inches, one-of-a-
kind, 2002 (specially
costumed version of
Carolyn and her doll;
shown in conjunction
with the 2002 UFDC
convention)

Butterfly Kisses Bethany,
vinyl, 12 inches, limited to 150,
2002 (special edition for the
2002 UFDC convention and first
souvenir made for UFDC by
Kish & Company; companion
outfit shown was also available
at event)

Liberty Belle and Freedom (from left), Club USA collection, vinyl, 16 inches and 12 inches, each limited to 300, 2002 (Liberty Belle nominated for a 2002 *Doll Reader* DOTY Award; Freedom is the Rachel doll)

Kaitlin and Kylie, vinyl (Kaitlin) and vinyl head, arms and legs with cloth body (Kylie), 12 inches and 4 ½ inches, limited to 20, 2003 (special edition for Happily Ever After)

Independence and Glory (from left), Club USA collection, vinyl, 16 inches and 12 inches, each limited to 300, 2002 (Independence is the Jo doll; Glory is Bethany)

Amber Waves, Unity and Justice (from left), Club USA collection, vinyl, 16 inches and 12 inches, each limited to 300, 2002 (Amber Waves is Bethany; Unity is Jo; and Justice is Christopher; Unity was shown on the cover of the July 2002 issue of *Dolls*)

Bebe, Lily and Evie (from left), Kishlets collection,
vinyl heads, arms and legs with cloth bodies, 4 ½ inches,
each limited to 500, 2003

Summer of Love, vinyl,
10 inches, limited to 100, 2002
(special edition for the 24th annual
Modern Doll Collectors'
Convention; Summer of Love is the
Sugar doll from 1993 done in a
pale skin color)

Peter Pan and
Tinkerbell, jointed
vinyl (Peter Pan)
and porcelain
head with cloth
body (Tinkerbell),
12 ½ inches and
4 inches, limited
to 12, 2002 (special
edition for the
Denver Doll
Emporium)

Bitty Bethany,
vinyl, 11 inches,
each limited to
500, 2003
(available in red,
brown or
blonde hair)

Global Kishlets, pencil on paper, 8 ½ inches by
11 inches, 2003

Evie, Bebe and Lily (from left), Global Kishlets,
vinyl heads, arms and legs with cloth bodies,
4 ½ inches, 2003

Electra, Facets of the Eternal Feminine
collection, vinyl, 16 inches, limited to
300, 2003 (introduced as the convention
souvenir for the 24th annual Modern Doll
Collectors' Convention)

Bitty Bethany, vinyl, 11 inches, limited to 500, 2004

IDEX Bitty Bethany, vinyl, 11 inches, limited to 25, 2004 (handpainted doll, special edition for 2004 IDEX show)

Belinda USA, vinyl, 12 inches, one-of-a-kind, 2004 (in the artist's personal collection)

Miss Bon Temps and Josiah, vinyl, 10 ½ inches and 10 inches, limited to 250 (Miss Bon Temps) and 10 (Josiah), 2003 (Miss Bon Temps was the souvenir doll for a 2003 UFDC luncheon in New Orleans; companion doll Josiah was sold separately)

Bitty Bethany in Tangerine Froth, Lime Sorbet and Falling Leaves ensembles (from left), 2004 (outfits were sold separately)

Bitty Bethany (in plaid) and Kishlet, Bitty and Itty collection, vinyl (Bitty Bethany) and vinyl head, arms, legs with cloth body (Kishlet), 11 inches and 4 ½ inches, set limited to 600, 2005

Bitty Belinda and Kishlet, Bitty and Itty collection, vinyl (Bitty Bethany) and vinyl head, arms, legs with cloth body (Kishlet), 11 inches and 4 ½ inches, set limited to 600, 2005

Bitty Bethany (in polka dots) and Kishlet, Bitty and Itty collection, vinyl (Bitty Bethany) and vinyl head, arms, legs with cloth body (Kishlet), 11 inches and 4 ½ inches, set limited to 600, 2005

Keepsake Bitty Bethany, vinyl, 11 inches, limited to 300, 2005 (special edition for the Keepsake Doll Club of New Jersey 2005 luncheon)

Blue Fairy Bitty Bethany, vinyl, 11 inches, limited to 30, 2005 (table centerpiece for the 26th annual Modern Doll Collectors' Convention)

Bitty Belle Magnifique, vinyl, 11 inches, limited to 750, 2006

Bitty Bethany Tres Chic, vinyl, 11 inches, limited to 750, 2006

Rio, Facets of the Eternal Feminine collection, vinyl, 16 inches, limited to 300, 2004

Electra, Facets of the Eternal Feminine collection, vinyl, 16 inches, limited to 300, 2004

Electra as Riley's Mom, vinyl, 16 inches, one-of-a-kind, 2005 (shown on the cover of the December 2005 issue of *Haute Doll*; created as a contest giveaway)

Electra in Pink, vinyl, 16 inches, one-of-a-kind, 2005 (Electra wears a costume designed by Tim Purk and made out of napkins)

IDEX Susie, vinyl, 8 inches, limited to 300, 2006 (special edition for the 15th anniversary of IDEX; Susie has the Riley face)

Debut Tamsin and Tamsin (from left), vinyl, 7 ½ inches, limited to 200, 2005 (Debut Tamsin) and limited to 350, 2006 (Tamsin) (Debut Tamsin was a special edition for Happily Ever After)

Electra as Pillar, vinyl, 16 inches, limited to 300, 2005 (special edition for the 2005 UFDC convention)

The Spirit of Summer, Facets of the Eternal Feminine collection, vinyl, 16 inches, limited to 500, 2006 (an interpretation of Electra)

The Spirit of Summer, watercolor pencil on paper, 11 inches by 14 inches, 2004

The Spirit of Autumn, Facets of the Eternal Feminine collection, vinyl, 16 inches, limited to 500, 2006 (an interpretation of Rio)

The Spirit of Autumn, watercolor pencil on paper, 11 inches by 14 inches, 2004

The Spirit of
Winter, watercolor
pencil on paper,
11 inches by
14 inches, 2004

The Spirit of Winter, Facets of the Eternal Feminine
collection, vinyl, 16 inches, limited to 500, 2006
(an interpretation of Electra)

The Spirit of Spring, Facets of the Eternal Feminine
collection, vinyl, 16 inches, limited to 500, 2006
(an interpretation of Rio)

The Spirit of Spring,
watercolor pencil on
paper, 11 inches by
14 inches, 2004

The Life of Riley

(From 2003)

Far from sophisticated (although she *does* attend a new-age preschool, she also wears ruffled jumpers and plays with chickens) and even farther from svelte (her rounded tummy protrudes shamelessly), Riley is not your typical fashion doll. Yet, Helen Kish's chubby-cheeked imp quickly became the darling of fashion-doll collectors soon after her debut in the summer of 2003.

One reason for Riley's instant popularity, says dollmaker Robert Tonner, is that she is "so darn cute!" That she is; what's more, the pint-sized prima donna is surrounded by a fast-growing group of equally cute chums. When you enter "Riley's World," be prepared to lose yourself to this vinyl thief of hearts and her merry band of cutie-patooties. Technically part of the artist's LadyKish Whimsies line, Riley's World has become so vast that it commands (or is it demands?) its own chapter.

Riley and Jingles, 2004 (costume and blue ribbon included in Riley and the Perfect Puppy Gift Set)

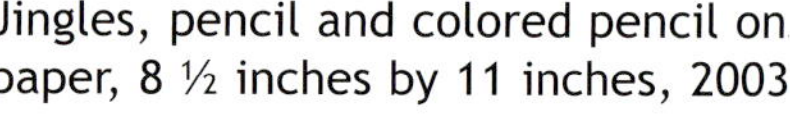

Jingles, pencil and colored pencil on paper, 8 ½ inches by 11 inches, 2003

Lavender Flower Fairy Riley, vinyl, 7 ½ inches, limited to 500, 2004 (special edition for the Kish Collectors' Society)

Riley, vinyl, 7 ½ inches, limited to 300, 2003 (introduced as a special edition for the annual UFDC convention)

Cheerleader Riley, vinyl, 7 ½ inches, limited to 50 (as a special edition for the Paris Fashion Doll Convention) and 250 (as a special edition outfit only for Collectors United), 2005

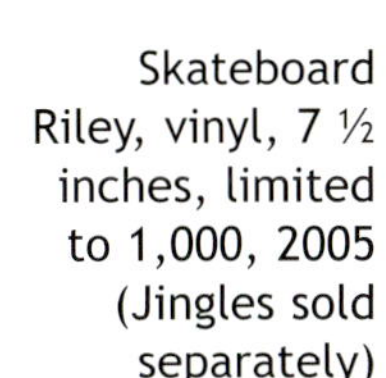

Skateboard Riley, vinyl, 7 ½ inches, limited to 1,000, 2005 (Jingles sold separately)

Riley and the Perfect Puppy Gift Set, vinyl (Riley) and resin (Jingles), 7 ½ inches and 2 3/4 inches, limited to 450, 2004 (shown on the cover of the September 2004 issue of *Dolls*; set included an extra costume and accessories)

Botanic Gardens Riley, vinyl, 7 ½ inches, limited to 1,000, 2004

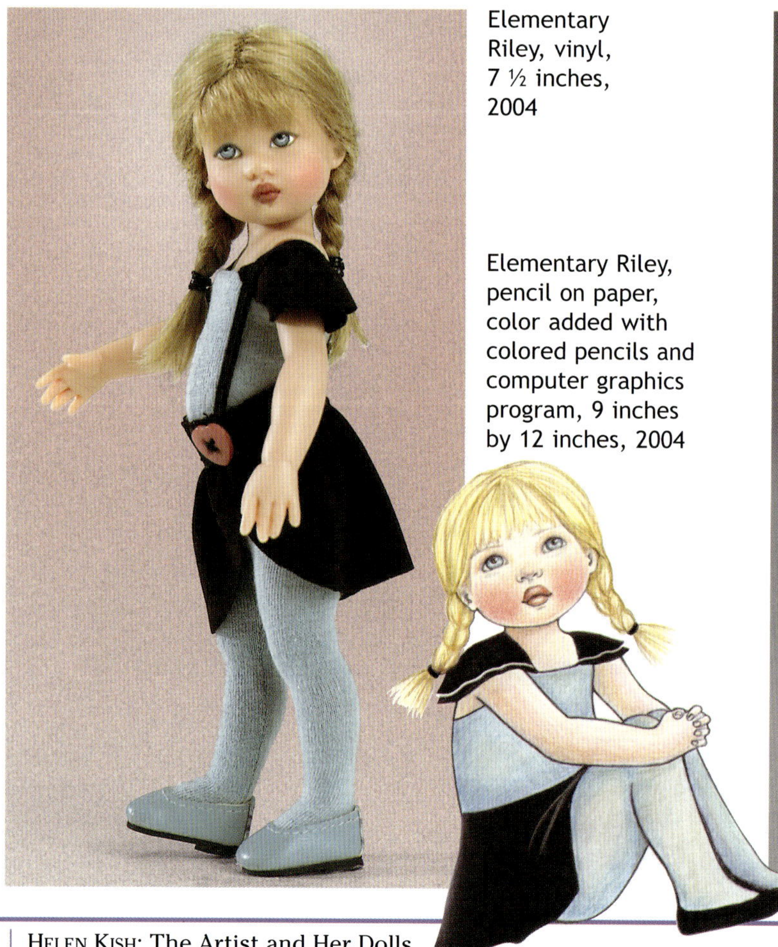

Elementary Riley, vinyl, 7 ½ inches, 2004

Elementary Riley, pencil on paper, color added with colored pencils and computer graphics program, 9 inches by 12 inches, 2004

Debut Tulah, vinyl, 8 inches, 2004 (special edition for the Kish Collectors' Society; shown in the background is the resin prototype)

Angelic Riley, vinyl, 7 ½ inches, limited to 1,000, 2004 (with Recital Tulah, shown on the cover of the November 2004 issue of *Contemporary Doll Collector*)

Riley in Chick Chic ensemble, 2004 (outfit only)

Tulah, vinyl, 8 inches, limited to 30, 2004 (centerpiece for the 26th annual Modern Doll Collectors' Convention; came with snack stand and umbrella)

Swimsuit Riley, vinyl, 7 ½ inches, limited to 800, 2005

Riley in Zen Garden Party ensemble, 2004
(outfit only)

Butterfly Riley, vinyl,
7 ½ inches, limited to
200, 2004 (special edition
for Collectors United)

Pink Ribbon
Riley, vinyl,
7 ½ inches,
limited to
1,000, 2005

Field Trip Riley, vinyl, 7 ½ inches, limited to 600, 2005 (gift set
came with carrying case, sleeping bag, night attire, Jingles the
dog and a crocheted hand puppet)

Baseball Riley, vinyl, 7 ½ inches, limited to 100, 2004 (special edition for the 25th annual Modern Doll Collectors' Convention; Tulah centerpiece doll is shown in background; outfit on Riley at left was also sold at the event)

Winter Riley, vinyl, 7 ½ inches, limited to 1,000, 2005

Club Riley, vinyl, 7 ½ inches, 2004 (special edition for the Kish Collectors' Society)

Club Riley, pencil on paper, color added with colored pencils and computer graphics program, 9 inches by 12 inches, 2004

Riley in exclusive outfit, New York, New York Riley, Dream Dolls Riley and Paris Riley (clockwise from lower left), vinyl, 7 ½ inches, 2004 (exclusive outfit) and 2005 (all other dolls) (exclusive outfit was a special edition for the Kish Collectors' Society; New York, New York was a special edition for Collectors United and limited to 300; Dream Dolls was a special edition for Dream Dolls Gallery and limited to 186; Paris was a special edition for the Paris Fashion Doll Convention and limited to 50)

Haute Riley, vinyl, 7 ½ inches, limited to 300, 2005 (special edition for *Haute Doll* magazine; shown on the cover of the December 2005 issue of *Haute Doll*)

UFDC Riley and UFDC Riley #2, vinyl, 7 ½ inches, limited to 300 (UFDC Riley) and 500 (UFDC Riley #2), 2004 (UFDC Riley) and 2005 (UFDC Riley #2) (special editions for UFDC)

North Pole Riley, vinyl, 7 ½ inches, limited to 500, 2005 (available only in a gift set from Reverie Publishing with Joan Muyskens Pursley's *Christmas Dolls* book)

Recital Riley, vinyl, 7 ½ inches, 2005

Recital Tulah,
vinyl, 8 inches,
2005

Haleena ("Hoop Dancer")
and Santa Fe Riley, vinyl,
7 ½ inches, limited to 300
(Haleena) and 200 (Santa Fe
Riley), 2005 (special editions
for the 2005 UFDC Region
3 Conference; Haleena is
the Anjali doll as a Native
American girl)

Field Trip Tulah, vinyl,
8 inches, limited to 600,
2005 (gift set came
with carrying case, sleeping
bag, nightgown, Toots
the kitten and other
accessories)

Anjali, vinyl,
7 ½ inches,
2005 (special
edition for the
Kish Collectors'
Society)

Ellery, resin,
6 inches, 2005
(Rolling Horse
sold separately)

Avery, vinyl,
8 inches, limited
to 1,500, 2005

Show and Tell Riley, vinyl, 7 ½ inches, limited to 1,000,
2005 (doll came with Jingles the dog, made with resin
head and cloth body)

Zsu Zse, vinyl,
7 ½ inches,
limited to 195,
2005 (souvenir for
the 2005 NIADA
conference)

DJ as Pinocchio,
vinyl, 8 inches,
limited to 200,
2005 (special
edition for the
26th annual
Modern Doll
Collectors'
Convention)

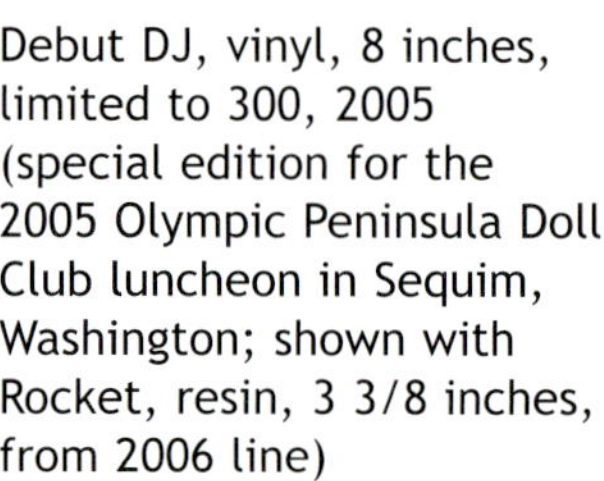

Debut DJ, vinyl, 8 inches,
limited to 300, 2005
(special edition for the
2005 Olympic Peninsula Doll
Club luncheon in Sequim,
Washington; shown with
Rocket, resin, 3 3/8 inches,
from 2006 line)

Club Zsu Zse, vinyl,
7 ½ inches, 2005
(special edition for
the Kish Collectors'
Society)

Riley in Casual Pink ensemble, 2005 (outfit only)

Tulah in Easter Egg ensemble, 2005 (outfit only)

Nurse Riley, vinyl, 7 ½ inches, limited to 1,000, 2006

Riley in Sweat Suit ensemble, 2005 (outfit only)

Fire Fighter DJ and Rocket, vinyl (DJ) and resin (Rocket) 8 inches and 3 3/8 inches, limited to 1,000, 2006

Concert Zsu Zse, vinyl, 7 ½ inches, limited to 1,000, 2006

Girls in Space Anjali, vinyl, 7 ½ inches, limited to 750, 2006

Raggedy Riley, vinyl, 7 ½ inches, limited to 1000, 2006

Toy Ellery, resin, 6 inches, limited to 650, 2006

Fancy Circus Tulah, vinyl, 8 inches, limited to 650, 2006

Explorer Avery, vinyl, 8 inches, limited to 650, 2006

Snow White Riley, vinyl, 7 ½ inches, limited to 500, 2006 (available only in a gift set from Reverie Publishing with the book *Helen Kish: The Artist and Her Dolls*)

Fiesta Riley, vinyl, 7 ½ inches, 2006
(available in two color schemes: pink
limited to 450; blue limited to 350)

Biographical Notes

1950: Helen Irene Nalty born September 18 in Denver, Colorado. Father, Donald Nalty; mother, Doris Nalty (Sillstrop)

1968: Graduates from Abraham Lincoln High School, Denver
Begins studies at the National College of Education, Evanston, Illinois

1969: Transfers to the University of Colorado at Boulder as art major

1970: Completes sophomore year at University of Colorado
Moves to New York City for the summer
Meets Tamas Kiss
Returns to Denver with Tamas Kiss in December

1971: Marries Tamas Kiss February 13

1972: Begins studies at the Rocky Mountain School of Art, Denver

1974: Begins work as an air-brusher
Makes first dolls, using synthetic clay (approximate year)

1975: Tamas Kiss becomes a US citizen; last name changed to Kish
Son Tomi born January 26
Makes Aimée, her first porcelain doll

1977: Son Ryan born March 30

1978: Accepted into the Original Doll Artists Council of America (ODACA; a juried organization for dollmakers)
Creates pivotal portrait doll of Uncle Don
Meets artist Martha Armstrong-Hand at the annual UFDC convention

1979: Daughter Annalise born February 25

1980: Newsboy shown on the cover of the March issue of *The Antiques Journal*

1981: Accepted into the National Institute of American Doll Artists (NIADA; a juried organization for dollmakers)
Artist and family move to new home in Littleton, Colorado

1983: Begins designing dolls for manufacturers and direct-mail companies (approximate year)

1985: Begins term as NIADA Standards Chairman (continues through 1988)
Meets artist Robert Tonner

1988: Victoriana shown on the cover of the March/April issue of *Dolls*

1991: Launches Kish & Company for the production of vinyl dolls
European Artist Dolls begins distributing/representing Kish & Company
Kelsey nominated for a *Dolls* Award of Excellence
Begins first of two terms as president of NIADA
First vinyl dolls—Kelsey, Mary Kate and Margie—ship at end of year

1992: Begins working with stoneware clay (approximate year)
Bust of Woman, porcelain, shown on the cover of *The Art of The Doll*, published by NIADA

1993: Sugar, Hannah and Andie shown on the cover of the September issue of *Contemporary Doll Magazine*

1994: Unveils The Sentinel, one of her earliest stoneware sculptures, at the 32nd annual NIADA conference

1995: The Little Match Girl wins *Dolls* Award of Excellence
Begins producing work in bronze (approximate year)

1996: Studies sculpting with Bruno Lucchesi, Loveland Academy of Fine Arts, Loveland, Colorado
Alice wins a *Dolls* Award of Excellence

1997: Adds first baby dolls, Carolyn and Elizabeth, to Kish & Company line

Studies sculpting for the second time with Bruno Lucchesi, Loveland Academy of Fine Arts, Loveland, Colorado
Charlotte shown on the cover of the September issue of *Miniatures*, a Spanish publication
Juliette and Emilie shown on the cover of the October issue of *Doll Reader*

1998: Artist and husband represent Kish & Company at Toy Fair in February, following split from European Artist Dolls
Collaborates with Robert Tonner on Sophie, the porcelain souvenir doll for the 36th annual NIADA conference

1999: Adds first vinyl adult, Isabelle Rose, to Kish & Company line
Isabelle Rose wins a *Dolls* Award of Excellence
Marisa wins a *Doll Reader* DOTY Award
Elizabeth and Carolyn shown on the cover of the June/July issue of *Dolls*
Creates Columbine Song, a dramatic stoneware work, to commemorate the Columbine High School killings of April 20

2000: Divides Kish & Company offerings into two arms: Signature Editions and LadyKish
Introduces Bethany, along with Christopher, Jo, Jack and Rachel
Bethany wins a *Doll Reader* DOTY Award
Marley and Kate shown on the cover of the August/September issue of *Doll*, a British publication
Kish Collectors' Society debuts

2001: Is selected by the Pleasant Company to sculpt the dolls in the Girls of Many Lands collection
Work published in *Here Come the Bride Dolls* (Portfolio Press) by Louise Fecher

2002: First dolls released in Pleasant Company's Girls of Many Lands collection
Lucy wins a *Doll Reader* DOTY award; Spectre de La Rose receives a nomination
Kiki and Cosette shown on the March cover of *Contemporary Doll Collector*
Introduces Butterfly Kisses Bethany, first souvenir made by Kish & Company for UFDC
Unity (Jo) from Club USA collection shown on the cover of the July issue of *Dolls*; Liberty Belle from same collection nominated for a *Doll Reader* DOTY award

2003: Family home, as well as Kish & Company headquarters, move to downtown Denver
Introduces Bitty Bethany, Electra and Riley
Kish & Company moves production to China
Renames LadyKish line as the LadyKish Whimsies

2004: Arabella and Cecily shown on the cover of the November/December issue of *Doll Castle News*
Introduces Tulah, friend of Riley
Work featured in *Dollmakers and Their Stories: Women Who Changed the World of Play* (Henry Holt and Co.) by Krystyna Poray Goddu

2005: Haute Riley and Electra as Riley's Mom shown on the cover of the December issue of *Haute Doll*
Introduces Anjali, Avery, Ellery, DJ and Zsu Zse, friends of Riley

2006: Debuts Raggedy Riley figurine collection

Bibliography

The following sources were consulted during the preparation of this text.

Fecher, Louise. "The Babies and Beauties of Helen Kish." *Dolls*, Vol. 7, March/April 1988, pp. 36-39.

_____. "Children are full of surprises . . . " In: News From the Studios, *Dolls*, Vol. 10, June/July 1991, p. 35.

_____. "Short Stops." In: News From the Studios, *Dolls*, Vol. 11, February/March 1992, p. 62.

_____. "New Vinyls from Helen Kish." In: News From the Studios, *Dolls*, Vol. 13, March/April 1994, p. 22

_____. "Helen Kish in porcelain, vinyl and stoneware." In: News From the Studios, *Dolls*, Vol. 13. December 1994, pp. 24-26.

_____. "Short Stops." In: News From the Studios, *Dolls*, Vol. 15, January 1996, p. 30.

_____. "Helen Kish's vinyl variety." In: News From the Studios, *Dolls*, Vol. 16, May 1997, pp. 26-27.

_____. "Keeping Up with Helen Kish." In: News From the Studios, *Dolls*, Vol. 19, September 2000, pp. 32-34.

_____. "Sealed With a Kish." *Haute Doll*, Vol. 2, November/December 2005, pp. 21-29.

Finnegan, Stephanie. "On a Lazy Afternoon." *Dolls*, Vol. 18, June/July 1999, pp. 72-75.

Goddu, Krystyna Poray. *Dollmakers and Their Stories: Women Who Changed the World of Play*. New York, NY: Henry Holt and Company, 2004.

_____. "When Children's Books Come Alive." *Dolls*, Vol. 18, June/July 1999, pp. 60-64.

_____. Interview with Helen Kish. October 4, 2002. [unpublished interview]

_____, ed. *The Art of the Doll: Contemporary Work of the National Institute of American Doll Artists*. N.p.: National Institute of American Doll Artists, 1992.

Matthews, Meredith. "Living the Life of Riley." *Dolls*, Vol. 23, September 2004, pp. 24-26.

Ryan, Kathleeen. "Decidedly Different: The Fine Arts Work of Helen Cunalta Kish." *Contemporary Doll Collector*, February/March 1999, pp. 40-47.

Witt, Kathy. "Dolls With Spirit." *Dolls*, Vol. 21, July 2002, pp. 40-43.

Index of Works